# How to Succeed as a Working Parent

**Steve Chalke**

Hodder & Stoughton
LONDON SYDNEY AUCKLAND

British Library Cataloguing in Publication Data
A record for this book is available from the British Library

ISBN 0 340 86120 7

Typeset in Garamond by Avon DataSet Ltd,
Bidford-on-Avon, Warwickshire

Printed and bound in Great Britain by
Clays Ltd, St Ives plc

The paper and board used in this paperback are natural recyclable products
made from wood grown in sustainable forests. The manufacturing processes
conform to the environmental regulations of the country of origin.

Hodder & Stoughton
A Division of Hodder Headline Ltd
338 Euston Road
London NW1 3BH
www.madaboutbooks.com

# Contents

# Acknowledgments

## Team Work

All achievement in life is, in the end, about being part of a team. Therefore, I am very fortunate in being part of several good teams who have contributed to this book.

Cornelia, Emily, Daniel, Abigail and Joshua (my wife and our four children) have patiently stuck with me as I've, all too slowly, struggled to get a grip on the principles outlined in these pages. My task here is to thank them for their constant generosity to a father for whom aspiration and achievement are so often separated by a huge gulf.

Then there is the team at Parentalk, working tirelessly behind the scenes, especially Maggie Doherty, Tim Mungeam and Sophia Hanvey who together developed the www.parentalk. co.uk/atwork website, and around which the content of this book is based. There would be no Parentalk without them.

A special mention must also be made of the team of working parents, Paul, Catherine, John, Daphne, Andy, Debbie, Stewart and Angela, who managed to find the time and the energy to contribute towards this project and so bring the chapters to life (this among all their other responsibilities!). I can vouch for the fact that each one truly is a hard-working parent.

Finally, a special thankyou to Alan Mann, who laboured long and hard over this manuscript with me – drafting and rewriting the material. Without him it would never have seen the light of day.

We hope that as you read the following pages you will feel that our labour has been worthwhile.

Steve Chalke
London, November 2002

# We're All Working Parents

A friend of mine was asked recently if becoming a parent had changed his life. His reply was simple. 'It's not so much changed it as completely ruined it!' Becoming a parent turns your life upside down. Before long every other aspect of how you spend your time and any other resources has to be reassessed in the light of this newfound commitment. Where you live; what you spend your money on; where you go on holiday; what car you drive; the hours you sleep; what you do in your free time (if you still have any!); the time you spend at work – and that's just for starters. Your child may be small and innocent to look at but – rather like one of those cute little *Gremlins* of Hollywood movie fame – they soon take over.

Being a parent is, of course, enormous fun, though it can also be extremely frightening. It is, at one and the same time, life's greatest joy and its biggest challenge. And though every child is unique, they all have one thing in common – not one of them ever asked to be born. Deliberately or not, we all invite our kids into our lives, which means that, once they've arrived, we *owe* them big time! From the moment they're born it's our responsibility to provide them with the generous and constant supply of time, security, love and care that they desperately need in order to truly thrive.

The problem is that sometimes it feels as though the combined pressures and demands of home and work are simply overwhelming. Instead of feeling like life's architect, you've ended up as one of its victims. You feel as though your offspring has taken over! As a friend of mine told me only last week, 'My son is just three and he's already the dominant personality in the house.' Or to change the metaphor, instead of enjoying the experience of sitting at the steering wheel of life, you feel as though you're stuck in its back seat as you hurtle, out of control, into the future. Even worse, you wonder if you have any real chance of ever managing to climb back into the driving seat again.

*How to Succeed as a Working Parent* is about retaking control. It is written for every mum and dad who finds themselves struggling to juggle with the competing demands of work and family life. And of course, in truth, every parent is a working parent – not only those in paid employment. So this book is for you whether your children are fifteen weeks or fifteen years old, whether you are married, live with a partner or face the responsibility of parenting alone. It is written for stepmums and stepdads, for parents who are fostering and for those who have adopted, for farmers and financial directors, for plumbers and PR consultants, for teachers and train drivers. It's even for you if you are one of those who are still at the stage of considering having a child but want to think about the implications in an informed way.

Whatever your situation you will find plenty of tried and tested advice in the pages that follow. What you won't find, however, is answers. The reason for this is simple – every parent/child relationship is unique, and so the solutions to the issues you face will be just as individual. So what you will find in this book is information . . . lots of it . . . as well as the key principles and questions to help *you* make the best choices for you and your child.

*How to Succeed as a Working Parent* is divided into ten chapters or 'Top Tips' (which are in turn split into three sections), filled with accessible, practical, thought-provoking and informative advice, which present you with the available options and alternatives, whatever your circumstances.

## Part One: Getting to Know the Real You

Focusing on how to find the right balance between work and home life

### Top Tip One: Get Your Values Straight
What do you really want for you and your family? How to make decisions about getting the balance right between home and work.

### Top Tip Two: Recognise the Tension
How to use the inevitable tension you feel between home life and work life in a positive and creative way.

### Top Tip Three: Deal with Guilt
Practical advice on how to deal with the guilt all parents feel from time to time. When do you listen, and when do you ignore it?

## Part Two: Taking Control

Focusing on practical ways to establishing a healthy work/life balance

### Top Tip Four: Budget Carefully

The thought of an evening spent poring over the figures is hardly everyone's idea of fun. But if you really want to sort out your work/life balance, being on top of your finances allows you to make better judgements about the options open to you.

### Top Tip Five: Talk to Your Employer

If, as a result of getting to understand the real you, you decide that you do want to change your working practices to benefit your family you are going to have to speak to your employer. So get yourself prepared by thinking through the issues from their perspective, as well as yours, before making your approach.

### Top Tip Six: Choose Childcare that You're Really Happy With

What are the options? What are the pros and cons? What are the big questions you should be asking before making your decision?

## Part Three: Making It Work

Focusing on the practical steps that will help you maintain that healthy balance between home and work long term

### Top Tip Seven: Make a Clear Division between Work and You

In our global, broadband, digital, contact-driven, 24/7 culture, where it's harder than ever to avoid the pressure to bring your work home with you or to extend the working day just that little bit longer again, the need to make a clear division between work and you is more important than ever. Your child needs to know when you're really available for them and when you're not. So just how should you go about it?

## Top Tip Eight: Remember Your Oxygen Mask
For any parent struggling to keep the balance between work and home, it's all too easy to find that your own 'space' has disappeared as a result. So how do you make time for yourself and keep your sanity?

## Top Tip Nine: Talk, Talk and Talk Some More
Being a parent is a trial-and-error business at the best of times. Life is often unbalanced, unplanned, unpredictable and chaotic. So where do you find the backup and support you need to make wise decisions in the midst of the battle?

## Top Tip Ten: Reassess Regularly
It makes sense to take a fresh look at things every now and then. What may have been a wonderful arrangement when your child was two years old will probably not be working quite as well by the time they are four, six, eight or twelve. So how do you keep ahead of the game and regularly monitor how you are doing?

With each of the ten Top Tips we've included some short sections given over to feedback and comment from a number of families, representing a range of social backgrounds and situations, who we asked to comment, in their own words, on the principles that we have set out in terms of how they apply to their day-to-day lives and routine. I hope that you'll be able to identify with some of the challenges they have faced and apply some of their ideas to your own situation.

Finally, if you have access to the Internet, you will find that www.parentalk.co.uk/atwork is packed with advice, resources and opportunities for discussion on everything you need to help you succeed as a working parent. And to help you to continue your quest on-line, the website is based around the same ten Top Tips as this book.

Enjoy!

Families featured in *How to Succeed as a Working Parent*

---

**Paul and Catherine** have three children, Luke (nine), Grace (six) and Titus (three). They have been married for ten years.

Parenthood has brought with it big changes to both Paul's and Catherine's work/home life balance – some of which were planned, some of which just happened!

Paul, thirty-seven (who has often toyed with the idea of becoming a house-husband), is currently the family's main breadwinner, enjoying the challenges of a senior job in the travel industry, which he took up recently. He and Catherine are aware, however, that work now impinges more on home life than before, with 24-hour on-call responsibilities, longer hours and occasional travel.

Catherine, forty (originally the more career-minded of the two), is at home full time, having taken a two-year career break from her job as an NHS manager. After first becoming a mum, she worked full time, then reduced to part time with baby number two, and job-shared, all with varying degrees of success. When baby number three came along, Catherine decided that it was time to take a 'break' and rethink her working life. She is now adapting to being at home and enjoying seeing more of the children (well, most of the time!).

---

**John**, thirty-eight, is a freelance cartoonist and comedy writer living in South London with his seven-year-old son, Pearse. John's wife is in the fashion business and lives for most of the year in Dublin, Ireland, frequently travelling from there to fashion shows in Europe and the USA. Several of her younger sisters live in London in the same house as John and Pearse. Pearse goes to school in London, so that John is his main carer, with support from in-laws, and during the summer months Pearse moves to Ireland to stay with his mum. Although Mum and Dad are physically apart for most of the year they are in constant phone contact and also travel back and forth between London and Dublin individually and with Pearse: 'Sometimes we think we see each other more often than people who live in the same house!'

**Andy and Debbie** are Mum and Dad to Sam (two). Debbie, thirty-three, is a qualified children's nurse and was required to return to work for two days a week when Sam was ten months old. It took her a long time to feel ready to become a mum, and she still sometimes thinks she is a better nurse than mother. She feels that working two days a week gives her the best of both worlds. Sometimes she would prefer to work more, especially when she is not coping well at home. Other times she really misses Sam when she goes to work but is so pleased to see him at the end of a busy day. For her, being a part-time working mum is a delicate balancing act, which requires a lot of communication, honesty and flexibility. When decisions have to be made she finds her priority always lies with her family.

Andy, thirty-four, has been self-employed as a website developer since Sam was one. He didn't find the transition to becoming a dad – or working from home with a mother and child never far away – easy to make but, looking back, working from home has been very helpful. Working for himself has given him a huge amount of flexibility and has enabled him to be able to help look after Sam and Debbie when they have been unwell or in need of a break.

**Daphne** has been on her own with James, now fourteen, since he was two years old. As the principal wage-earner she went back to work, full time, when James was nine weeks old.

When he was nine years old she negotiated a part-time contract at work and for the next eighteen months spent more time with James and saw him into senior school. That worked well and she returned to full-time work two years ago. Now, with James' GCSEs looming, Daphne is reassessing her priorities in order to see him through the next critical years of his education.

**Angela and Stewart** are married with four children, two from Angela's previous relationship: James (eighteen), Naomi (seventeen), Denise (thirteen) and Vanessa (eleven). Denise is hyperactive and has chronic epilepsy and brain damage, and Naomi has epilepsy, asthma, diabetes, bowel, bladder and eating problems, and high blood pressure.

Stewart is Acting Garage Support Assistant at Brixton bus garage. Angela volunteers part time at their local carers' centre and enjoys helping and talking to people.

They both used to be in scouting but gave it up due to family pressures. When they have the time, Stewart enjoys reading – he's especially got into Tolkien books recently – and computing. Angela enjoys entertaining, Catherine Cookson books, relaxing in front of a video and collecting dolls.

They met when Angela's parents moved to Hove to start a caretaking job at a church. Stewart was in the youth group there, and met Angela when she came down to visit her parents. He'd been looking for a partner but managed to find one with a built-in family!

**Part One**

# Getting to Know the Real You

# Get Your Values Straight

## Take an honest look at yourself

Nicholas was hugely successful. He was extremely smart, well educated, at the top of his profession; well connected, very well paid and lived the lifestyle of a king. He had everything you could ever want. And yet he was one of the unhappiest men I ever met – the classic victim of his own success, living out a life that had taken years of hard work to achieve but at the expense of the one thing he claimed to cherish most – his family. If asked the question, 'What is the most important thing in your life?' he would be quick to reply, 'My children.' But if you asked his friends, or most importantly his family, they'd all tell you a very different story. What was absolutely clear to everyone was that his career, money, fame and success were what mattered most to him and that what he said and what he did just didn't stack up.

For years his work kept him away from home from Sunday evening through to Friday afternoon and his wife and his children, who were in their early years, only ever saw him at weekends. But when the opportunity came to work even harder he simply couldn't resist it and began to work weekends as well, fitting his family in when he could – usually only during holidays. The greatest tragedy, however, is this – by the time Nicholas had grown tired of chasing the pound, status and promotion and instead decided to 'be there' for his family, they had grown tired of waiting. His children had grown older and his wife had grown colder. They had waited so long for Nicholas to be around and enjoy life with them that they had slowly given up hope. By the time Nicholas had realised what he had missed it had gone, and his children had grown up and moved on.

Nicholas' story is an extreme example, but the truth is that every working parent has to face the same difficult question at one level or another: How do you balance a working life with raising a family?

Children, especially very young ones, place huge demands on their parents' time. And this need for time is equally as great as that of bread on the table, clothes on their back and a roof over their head. Having a child may open you up to a whole set of new wonders in life, but it also forces you to take a very long sobering look at the values you hold and the lifestyle you lead. And trying to avoid the issues now means they will only be back to bite you hard in years to come. The simple truth is you can't avoid them so – instead of trying – put your thinking cap on and be honest with yourself about you, your family and your need to work (which may be linked to finance or fulfilment). And be prepared to take the necessary action to achieve it. For some, there will not be much need for debate. Many mums and dads have no option but to work full time to make ends meet. They work from necessity rather than choice. But for others there are choices.

---

**Daphne** (single mum to James, works full time):

This issue has evolved as James has grown up. I really had no choice when he was a baby – we needed a roof over our heads, the bills had to be paid and, fortunately, I enjoyed my job. Added to which, I had a superb, fully qualified, live-in nanny who stayed with us until James was four years old. The main pressure was external, when people used to ask if James thought the nanny was his mother. That hurt. I chose an excellent nanny; we both knew the ground rules. She was a great support to James – even through the tricky business of a divorce.

As James neared the end of junior school I felt the need to be with him more, and to help prepare him for senior school. It was pretty scary to come out of my comfort zone at work and become part time. What a great decision it was! Collecting him from school and having the time to kick a football around on the heath – money could never buy that. I look back with very fond memories.

Fortunately James took to senior school like a duck to water and when my employer asked if I could work five days a week again, the timing was perfect. I went back happily, with no detrimental effect on James. We still had a nanny and she stayed living with us until James was eleven years old.

I constantly have to review my values and with GCSEs looming it's another opportunity to consider what will be best for us. Working out a way to spend more time at home for James is the next big challenge. Money is pretty high up on a teenager's list of requirements so I need to be clear about my own (non-monetary!) values that will benefit us both.

---

Ask yourself:

- Do I want to work for financial reasons?
- Do I need to work for financial reasons?
- Can I manage on a part-time salary or will I have to work full time?
- Do I want to work for other reasons – self-fulfilment, self-worth, mental stimulation, etc.?
- Will my partner also need to go on working?
- What affect will these arrangements have on my child?

Of course, part of your response to these questions may well be based as much on your love or loathing of the work you do as it is on the practicalities of bringing up a child. Though work for some is simply about providing for their family, others get far more from being employed to do a job than simply a pay cheque at the end of the month. One of the main driving forces behind the feminist movement of the 1960s and 1970s wasn't the argument that women *needed* to work but that women *wanted* to work beyond the confines of the home. Freedom, equality, purpose, self-fulfilment – all these and many more are the reasons why we drag ourselves from our beds every morning and off to our place of employment. It's because so much of our identity is tied up with our occupation that we often choose to work even when we don't have to. Let's face it, if spending power is the only great benefit of employment why do so many people choose to do voluntary work? As someone once observed, 'We work to become, not to acquire.'

But while our identity might be wrapped up in our work, for a parent, it is also inextricably linked with their relationship with their child. Employers are fast catching up with the idea that their employees are more than just names on the payroll and that making provision for the fact that they are also often parents is an important part of the employment package. As a result, the world of work for many parents is fast becoming a world of options. A growing number of companies now have some form of paternity as well as maternity leave and increasingly employers offer incentives like flexi-hours, career breaks and crèches. While we may be a long way from a utopia for working mums and dads, things are a great deal easier than they were even a decade ago.

But having options, the choice to work full time or part time, to take a career break or extended maternity leave, means that now, more than ever, every parent has to think about their values. Gone are the days when 'the wife' was expected to stay at home to look after the kids while her husband, 'the breadwinner', went out to earn an honest day's pay. For the vast majority of us, children and work are part of the complex juggling act of life in the twenty-first century. So how important is your career? How important is being at home with your child? What choices are realistically available to you? There are no easy or right and wrong answers to these questions but, if we are going to succeed as working parents, then our walk is going to have to match our talk. Are you saying one thing but doing another? We all need to take an honest look at ourselves, not only for our own sakes but also, more importantly, for our children.

---

**Catherine and Paul** (married with three children – Paul works full time, Catherine is on a career break)

**Catherine**: When we were expecting our first child, there was no question in my mind that I would give up work and look after our baby at home, probably 'until he went to school'. I'm sure I was influenced by my own childhood when Dad went out to work and Mum was always 'there' for us. I envisaged this rosy picture of Paul going to the office and me becoming the efficient but calm and creative mum and homemaker! It didn't cross my mind that work was an important part of me and that I would be twitching without

---

it. My pregnancy had been stressful at work due to long hours and pressures in the office – I was delighted to be escaping into a new world! Paul was happy to go along with this (he obviously envisaged the same rosy picture) – although he would have equally been happy to try being at home himself for a while, an idea which I quickly dissuaded him from.

We thought we'd just about be able to cope on one salary, but in truth we didn't really look at this carefully enough and we were caught out later. I took maternity leave to keep my options open and, in the end, I was extremely glad that I had.

After Luke was born, it took me a while to emerge from the initial hazy elation of having a new baby. He was a beautiful and very peaceful boy (I was lucky; number two was equally beautiful but not quite so peaceful!). Being a mum was lovely, but the reality was not what I'd expected. I loved the sense of motherly fulfilment, but in all honesty I started to miss working. My brain was under-stimulated and I was really at sea without the regular contact of adults outside my baby-centred world.

I tried hard to make the most of being at home, joining music groups and just about every toddler group on offer – I even helped run one. It was a busy schedule and I began to realise that it was me who was craving activity – Luke's needs were far more basic.

We first realised that we needed to re-evaluate the stay-at-home option when I started telling Paul how to do his job – so hungry was my brain for office activity! Then we ran out of money!

Once back at work, with Luke happily settled with a live-out nanny, I felt more like me again, although my attitude to work had changed as it has for almost every new parent I know. However interesting things were at the office, getting home to see Luke in the evening was much better.

Looking back, we agree that we didn't evaluate too well and consider all the choices available. I was obsessed with not being out of the workplace for too long and felt I needed to get back on track quickly in case I became unemployable. Now I think this was ridiculous – I could have considered working part time earlier and/ or perhaps looked for a local job, even if that meant less seniority and money for a time. By going straight back into full-time work and commuting, etc. I missed out on some of our son's early years, as people kept warning me I would.

We did learn, though, to evaluate better with our second and third children and I'd advise others not to rush into things and never to accept second best unless there is no choice. We found we needed to look honestly at what we ideally wanted for our family first, then consider all the options and limitations before trying to bring it all together into something that was as near as possible what we really wanted.

## If you value your child then value time

In January 2002 the world of business and finance was shocked when the chief executive of one of Britain's biggest companies announced that he was quitting his £340,000-a-year job to spend more time with his wife and four children. Danny O'Neil decided that having missed out on seeing his eldest daughter grow up he wasn't about to make the same mistake with his nine-year-old triplets. His wife, Patricia, also decided that the time had come for her to give up work as a practice nurse.

Danny O'Neil didn't have an average job. He earned a salary that most of us can only ever dream of. However, as working parents, both he and his wife still had to assess their values and make some tough decisions. We all live the lifestyle that our income will allow us to. Although their income created a significant buffer, Danny and Patricia still faced many of the same questions and choices as you and I do. But even though by deciding to halve his salary and work just three days a week, Danny might have faced a slashed 'benefits package', in many ways his 'bonuses' will have increased in incalculable ways. The truth is, in giving up his dream of being a high-flying executive, Danny O'Neil and his wife Patricia communicated to their children in a very tangible way that *they* were the priority – not material gain, career-ladder-climbing or the pursuit of self-importance. When their children become old enough to have families of their own, their role model for family life won't be a working mum and an absent father providing them with plenty of possessions but never being there to share their lives. Instead, they will remember parents who put them first and paid the price, who demonstrated their love, not in gifts, but in the giving of precious time.

Any child would get a buzz from being dropped off at school in the latest chauffeur-driven executive saloon once or twice, but the reality is that your child would much rather arrive on a regular basis in an old banger driven by *you* than any other vehicle in the world. Your child's built-in 'love-ometer' isn't swung by the amount or quality of material possessions you can supply them with but rather by the amount of time that you invest in them, by the interest you take in them and in building a relationship with them. That's because every child spells love T-I-M-E. And it's not just love that gets passed on when you spend time with your child, but your values also.

The experts tell us that the average dad spends just three minutes a day in 'quality' conversation with his kids. The average mum does slightly better, knocking up five and a half minutes. By contrast, the average child spends three hours a day watching TV. So it doesn't take Einstein to work out who has the major influence on many kids' lives. And it's not just the TV that shapes their morals and beliefs. School, music, magazines, computers, radio, books, advertising, videos, other adults, pressure groups and friends all form the constant barrage of views and values that your child sees and hears every single day. Children are like sponges: they soak up their values from the influences around them. So even if you are not influencing them, lots of other people are. In fact, if you're not influencing your child, you're about the only person in their life who isn't. Whether you end up working part time, full time or not at all, if you want your child to grow up with values worth having and a strong sense of security, spending time with them must be your highest priority.

---

**Andy and Debbie** (Mum and Dad to Sam – Andy works from home, Debbie is a part-time nurse)

**Debbie**: I had always thought that I would work part time after having children. I had always wanted us to have the largest influence on Sam during the early years. However, I have found motherhood far tougher and more demanding than ever a busy shift as a children's nurse at the hospital! I think it's partly because I am a people person. It has become easier now that I am able to communicate with Samuel who is twenty-two months old. At times I thought that Samuel was having a happier time at nursery than at home with me but I have had to learn to grab every opportunity to meet with other mothers and do activities with other people during the week. I have found that being back at work has helped me gain the confidence I had lost during the ten months after Sam was born. think that I appreciate the time I spend with Samuel a lot more since I have been back to work. I still feel that Andy and I should have the most influence on Samuel, and the more time we spend with him the more this happens naturally. It really is about finding a balance. I am not someone who would cope with being the main parental influence with a partner who works long hours. For us sharing the roles of parent and income-earner is how we have learned to cope most effectively as parents, professionals and partners.

## What values do you want your child to inherit?

The reality is that most of the values you pass on to your child will come from the way you live rather than the things you say. When it comes to our children, we teach our best lessons without moving our lips. You can spend as many years as you like giving your child the latest version of your *big values talk*, but sooner or later you will realise that 'Do as I say, not as I do' never works. It's simply not the way children learn. Children are mimics. If you don't believe me sit your child down in front of the TV for an hour and watch their response. Whether it's the *Teletubbies* or the *Tweenies*, *Neighbours* or *EastEnders*, *Top of the Pops* or an action movie, it won't be long before they will be copying what they see and taking on board what they hear. In the same way they slowly pick up from you their concepts of right and wrong, how to relate to others and what's important in life.

Hollywood often uses tragedy to emphasise a point. In the film *Dead Poets Society*, the story is told of the relationship between a rather stern but well-meaning father and his teenage son. Neil's dad constantly pushes him to succeed – to get good grades and become a doctor: a good, stable, prestigious job. His idea of success is couched in academic achievement, financial gain and social status – after all, according to him, that's what's important in life. The son, however, encouraged by Mr Keating, his English teacher, has his heart set on being an actor, which is a far more risky, poorly paid and often short-term career. Success for him is about being happy, following his heart, friendship, trust, loyalty and love.

To make him focus on his studies, Neil's father bans him from taking part in all out-of-school activities. But Neil secretly auditions for a local production of *A Midsummer Night's Dream*. He's extremely talented and lands one of the lead roles in the play. When his dad finds out, he's furious. Though he loves his son immensely, and only wants the best for him, he's absolutely convinced that this has to mean becoming a doctor. After he's qualified, Neil can do what he likes with his spare time. In the meantime, what he needs most is something to knock this silly passion for acting out of him and focus his mind on his studies once and for all. So he decides to take Neil out of his strict and regimented school and send him to an even stricter and *more* regimented one!

The problem is that, as far as Neil is concerned, it seems that his dad will love him only on the condition that he stops being himself. Why can't he just accept him for who he is? Finally, when Neil realises that his dad will never let him become an actor, he spirals into depression, which ends with him tragically taking his own life with his father's gun. His reasoning is simple: if his dad can't love him as he is, with no strings attached, it means he can't really love him at all. And since Neil desperately needs his dad's love and approval in order to cope with life, he can't see a way forward.

Of course, this is only a film – a fictional portrayal of a parent/child relationship. But the truth is that it's a scenario that is played out to a lesser degree the length and breadth of the country, every day of the year. It's not that encouraging your child to do well at school is a bad idea in itself; it is simply that if they begin to believe that the only way to be a success is to get the highest grades at school, to win awards and be the best, then you are setting them up for an inevitable sense of failure. More than that, in later years, there's also the very real danger that they will end up focusing on career-climbing in order to try and achieve self-worth at the expense of their own family. The truth is that it's all too easy to set in motion a vicious circle of twisted values that will be passed from parent to child, to grandchild, to great-grandchild, etc.

Though there are some parents who consciously or otherwise try to make up for their own failures and unfulfilled dreams by pushing their children to succeed in their place, for the vast majority of us our only motive is what's best for our child. We want to see them happy and fulfilled, and we naturally want them to do well. So we push them to work hard. There's nothing wrong with this, of course. In fact, if we didn't push them at all, they'd begin to wonder if we *cared* how they turned out. A bit of pressure and challenge is good for them. But it's a delicate balance, because *too much* pressure is crippling. Rather than being constructive, it becomes very destructive.

---

**John** (Dad to Pearse, works from home while his wife works abroad):

Both as a cartoonist and a comedy writer for TV and books, I've always worked pretty much in the area of family entertainment, so I've been nodding my head at all the values that Steve mentions in this first chapter. Both before and after I became a parent, I think these strong family values were very much reflected in my work. However, when I did become a parent it was quite a shock to realise that it was one thing to write family values into a script or book manuscript . . . it's quite another thing to put them into practice in a real family situation.

I guess I've always realised I'm pretty lucky in being able to make a career out of something I very much enjoy – in fact when people

---

ask me if I'm doing what I wanted to do when I grew up, I tell them I'm still waiting to grow up. It's a nice line . . . but perhaps not as amusing to a child who needs a strong parental role model to lead the way, or to my wife left to fend for herself with a teething baby while I was waiting to be heckled off down the Fool and Firkin comedy club. Was I a complete hypocrite? Honestly, no . . . I passionately believed in the family values I was writing about. However, like many creative people in exciting jobs, I had fallen for the myth that if I just worked hard enough, focused exclusively enough and generally put every other aspect of my life on hold, I'd someday get the big break, the magic contract, the once-in-a-lifetime opportunity that would bring all the success and finances I would need to get the rest of my life in order, save my marriage and make time for my kid.

Now I've worked with enough showbiz legends to know that this scenario ain't never gonna happen – either the mythical 'big break' never shows up, or it finally does show up, only your partner and kids have got tired of waiting and moved on long ago, leaving you all dressed up but with absolutely no place to go spiritually or emotionally. My own life was certainly riding for that kind of fall, when my wife Fumi who works in the fashion business had to move overseas to work. Since one of the perks of being a freelance is that my time is a lot more flexible for school runs , etc., I went from being the absent parent to our child's main carer in one fell swoop. Now, my wife is still a very 'hands on' parent to our son Pearse; we liaise on the phone constantly about his welfare and schooling and he spends summer holidays in Ireland with her . . . but having to get my own hands 'dirty' at the business end of parenting has made all the difference to my life.

Much to my amazement, since putting family before career, not only has my family life blossomed but my career has too, perhaps because I give it a bit less than my all, and take it slightly less seriously. Come to think of it, the big break did show up after all – just not from the direction I was expecting.

Think about what values you've inherited from your own parents, good and bad. The chances are the values you would want to pass onto your own children will be things like generosity, patience, honesty, commitment, love, integrity – the kind of values that will make them good people to be around. So, with all that in mind, hold a mirror up to your life and take a long hard look at yourself. If you don't like what you see then do something about it.

When a couple I know became parents they decided that it was important to spend some time reflecting on the values they wanted to live by and to pass on to their daughter, and how their working practices might impact these. Naturally their thoughts started with their own experiences of home life and how their own parents handled the pressures of work and bringing up a family. Peter was particularly challenged about thinking through the amount of time he needed to spend working in relation to the time he wanted to spend with his new daughter.

'Inevitably my thoughts went back to how I grew up and how often I saw my own father,' Peter remarked. 'Back then, in some respects, things were far more difficult if you wanted to spend time with your family. There wasn't the same flexibility in the labour market, and you certainly didn't get any paternity leave. I decided that I did not want to be the kind of father who goes out in the morning with marmalade on his suit following a rushed breakfast, and then returns sometime around bath-time, too tired to play with my children. I wanted a richer life than that.'

Both Peter and his wife thought long and hard about all the implications of scaling down the hours that he worked. In the end they decided that the best option was for them to both work part time. Doing so has meant that they are able to share the joy of bringing up their daughter. They both now get much more time not only to spend with her but with each other – hopefully being the biggest and most positive influence on her as she grows, living out their values and instilling in her a set of values to equip her for life.

---

**Angela and Stewart** (Stewart works shifts, Angela is at home full time, they have four children, two from Angela's previous relationship)

**Angela**: When Stewart and I were having our first child together, I already had James who was four and a half, nearly five, and Naomi, who is disabled and has special needs, who was nearly four. I'd already lost some babies due to late miscarriage and other things. I had a stressful pregnancy, having to go in and out of hospital.

When I was about five months' pregnant I had to go into hospital, due to the baby not putting weight on. That was very hard to do. Stewart and I were worried and we knew that Stewart could not get much time off work as he had just started a new job. Friends all helped us.

Stewart and I talked a lot about me working part time. It would be very hard for me to do that with Stewart's hours at work and myself having to go to the hospital for check-ups with Naomi and other appointments. We did not have our parents nearby and it was very hard making the right decision. I wanted to be at home with the children but I didn't want Stewart to just be a part-time dad.

Stewart was working as a milkman and getting up very early in the morning, so we decided that he would not have to get up in the night to feed Denise. Denise was a hard baby. She never slept and she was always being sick after her feeds. So on a Saturday night Stewart did the night feed and got up with her, so I could have one night's sleep. We still do it now when Denise is bad at night. Stewart does the night run so I can have a night's sleep. With my health problem it is better for us that I stay at home.

---

## Remember

- Even when you feel powerless to change your work situation, you may still have options open to you.
- Children spell love T-I-M-E.
- Children soak up their values from influences around them.
- Things that you think your child views as important may not be – it may be more of a reflection of *your* personality than theirs.

## Key principle

**Get your values straight – the things that are most important to you – for your own sake and your child's. You are a role model, whether you like it or not!**

## How to achieve it

- Take an honest look at your own values.
- Aim to be the sort of person you want your child to become.
- If you have a partner, talk together honestly about the things that are important to you.
- Decide, as a parent, how important a part work plays in your life and take things from there.
- Face up to any pressing issues now – delay will only add to them.
- Whether you work or not, make spending time with your child top of your list of priorities.

# Recognise the Tension

'We aren't all naturals at this parenting game. And why on earth should we be? The biggest problem is that children don't come with easy-to-follow manuals. They don't even come in standard packages, for goodness sake! My youngest has turned out to be bewilderingly different from my eldest. Just when I thought I had at least got the early years sussed it was back to the drawing board.'

My friend Laura, part-time marketing consultant and full-time mother, is absolutely right. Being a parent is a steep learning curve and an experience that all the planning and advice in the world can never truly prepare you for. Not only is every child different, but every stage of their growth into adulthood brings fresh challenges that need to be taken on board and responded to in order to maintain a healthy balance between work and home, for both you and your child.

Every parent who, whether through choice or necessity, has to learn to balance work life with home life will readily identify the tension that exists as they try their best to cope with the relentless demands of both. When we first launched our website – www.parentalk.co.uk – we carried out some research looking at whether mums and dads felt they were getting the right balance between work and home. It was very clear from the results that achieving and then managing to maintain that balance is immensely difficult for everyone. But while there may be no way to escape this tension, there are ways to stop it overwhelming you and even of getting it to work for you as you develop good work and family relationships. The rest of this chapter takes a look at five key principles that could just make all the difference for you.

## 1. The tension is your friend

If there's one word that sums up life in the twenty-first century that word is *stress*. 'If only I had less pressure. If only I had a better job, could pay off the credit card bill, get the children into a better school, afford a big house, drive a newer car, find more time for myself, relax more and worry less.' Life can seem like nothing more than a frantic juggling act, coping with countless pressures and living from one crisis to the next. But though too much stress is bad for us, a bit of pressure can also be a very good thing.

The stress you feel is your friend. Stress is an in-built defence system. The right level of stress is empowering. It makes us more productive and efficient. In fact, a life without any stress or pressure is no use to anyone. But too much stress sets off our internal warning bell and the message is simple – slow down before you break down.

Stress, like physical pain, is designed to help us see when things need attention. If you stand in the kitchen having a conversation and casually lean back onto the hot hob, there's no doubting that the pain you will feel will motivate you to take immediate, remedial reaction! The pain you feel, though unwelcome, is actually a gift. Without it the consequences of your action could be disastrous. The same is true of stress; when it motivates us to take action, it's a good thing.

The real problem is not that we feel stress but that too often we try to grin and bear it instead of listening to it and taking action to reduce its impact on our families and us. Remember, honesty is the better part of valour. Keeping a stiff upper lip has been massively overrated. Feeling the tension does not mean you are failing. Real failure is to ignore the warning signs and allow stress to take control and begin to have a detrimental effect on you and your family.

A few years ago I was asked to visit Northern Ireland to speak at some seminars on parenting. On arrival at the airport my host was there to meet me. The welcome was extremely warm and friendly. 'Are you looking forward to this, Steve?'

I thought for a second. I knew that the right, encouraging and professional answer should have been a buoyant 'yes'. The reality, however, was that I was tired and missing my wife and

children already. 'Actually,' I sheepishly replied, 'I'd rather be at home with my family.' I felt awful and instantly regretted my reply.

But instead of being struck dumb by my reply, the honesty of it had reassured him that I lived with the tension of being a working parent in the same way he did. I was shocked at my host's response. 'That's great, Steve, it's what I expected and at least I know now that you will be worth listening to.'

The truth is, if I had tried to give the impression that I didn't struggle with these same issues he would have been worried that I was a remote and uncaring father as well as an unsuitable speaker.

The fact that you feel the pressure of being a working

parent is a sign that you *do* care, not that you don't. So don't be hard on yourself. It's normal, natural and even healthy to feel the tension of your competing responsibilities. You will spend your life working to get and then keep right the balance between work and home. Welcome this tension as a friend in your ongoing quest to achieve your goal.

---

**Catherine and Paul** (married with three children – Paul works full time, Catherine is on a career break)

**Catherine**: We've found, on the whole, that trying to get the work/life balance right has become more of a challenge as we've had more children. In the big juggling act, there are just more balls to juggle and more to drop! I certainly feel as if I've dropped a ball from time to time but I'm sure I'm not alone in that.

After we had our second baby, I had been promoted and felt I was spread so thinly that the quality of my work suffered as well as my time at home with Paul and the children. I was trying to give 100 per cent to my family and 100 per cent to work and the result was tiredness and feelings of guilt and inadequacy – not a recipe for success or contentment.

Once I started working part time, some (but not all!) of the tension was eased. Job-sharing really worked for me – it allowed me to split my time realistically between work and home. Three days at work and four to throw myself into the family seemed about right.

Even with the 'perfect' working arrangement, there was still that 'lack of control' feeling as a parent. Even now I find it difficult to let go and accept that it's just the way it is and it's like that for everyone.

One of the things that I found caused me the most tension was when the children were ill. That stress-knot in my stomach when they were sick late on Sunday – that anticipation of the call to tell colleagues that I wouldn't be in the next day. I've always felt bad and feel the need to overcompensate for hours missed. It helps me to remember that from time to time almost everyone has to have time off – parent or not. The most important thing is to demonstrate long term that you are a reliable and conscientious worker who doesn't want to let anyone down.

Using time off carefully is one way we've tried to limit the tension caused by juggling parenting and working. We always try to devote time off to being together and doing things as a family so our children see that time with them is important to us.

Even time off can present tensions – I get so stressed by trying to juggle 'quality' time with the children and doing the domestic tasks that come with family life. I know having a tidy and clean house is not as important as having healthy and happy children, but living in a mess is stressful and my stress tends to affect the whole family! When I was working we employed a cleaner for a few hours a week – I relaxed more about the house and there was more family time available.

Because we've decided to focus weekends, etc. on the children, we haven't stuck to the original timetable for renovating our house – also, we're hopeless at DIY! After five years, we still have bare floorboards upstairs (and I don't mean polished ones), the kitchen cupboard door is still off and there are no proper curtains at our bedroom window.

We've resisted taking on 'extra' things while our children are still relatively young. I don't mean we don't commit ourselves to anything, but we try not to take on an extra burden because we feel we ought to. For us, that means we're happy to have some responsibilities in other community activities – we want to be involved and find it rewarding. But for the foreseeable future, I am leaving the toddler group and school fete confidently in the hands of others who have the time and flair to do them brilliantly.

## 2. Get organised

Most of us are used to organising our working day with the precision of a military manoeuvre – appointments are made (and kept), decisions are reached, deadlines are worked to (well, most of the time!) and so on. The reason is simple – we know that there will be a big price to pay if we are inefficient. At home, however, it's a different story. Even though the price for inefficiency here may be less tangible, it's arguably far greater. Failing to keep your home commitments sends a clear and devastating message to your child – that they are simply not high enough on your list of priorities to matter. Although the very fact that you are reading this book means that this is not true, that's the message you send. The reality is, it's more a lack of organisation than a lack of love that keeps us from spending the time that we'd like to with our children. But though our problem might be more 'woodenness' than 'wicked-ness' – the truth is, it's just as damaging.

So here's the challenge – to start organising your home life with the attention that you devote to your work life. It needn't reach the levels of 'I've pencilled in your bedtime story for two weeks on Tuesday, OK?' but at the same time don't feel that blocking time in your diary for your child is far too prescriptive a move. Committing yourself to family time is an extremely smart move to make. But having done so, learn to be flexible – sometimes it comes off, sometimes not. Remember, if you don't plan, it never will! Of course, when children are younger they are always there, which makes things straightforward when it comes to fitting them into your diary. But as they get older you will discover that though you're available they often aren't. So keep booking that time in while you have the opportunity. The day is coming fast when they won't be around at all. Then you'll look back on these days and long to relive the opportunities you have right now. Don't throw any of them away and never forget that spontaneity takes a lot of organising!

All this talk of setting aside time may seem a little extreme. Perhaps you are one of the lucky ones whose job fits nicely into a nine-to-five – you work locally, with no overtime, no unsociable hours and no necessity to take work home with you. But don't get complacent. There are big dangers in assuming that this means that you are guaranteed to be spending lots of quality time with your children.

For much of my working life I've had to be away from home for days or occasionally even weeks at a time. It's simply a necessary aspect of the work I do. And many times, while on the road, I've stayed with other families where the parents have found it difficult to even consider the possibility of being away from their children for a night. In fact, I don't think I could count the number of times I've heard mums or dads tell me that they could never be away from their kids like I have to be. 'How do I cope?' they often ask.

Naturally I am extremely aware that my wife and my children miss out when I'm not around, and I know that I do too. But this stark situation has made me very conscious that I need to work hard at giving time back to my family whenever I am around – to make sure they know that they are a big priority for me, that I love them and that *they* are the centre of my life, not my job. And ironically, I've often noticed that those same parents who couldn't bear to be away from their children often fall into a huge trap: Being around isn't the same as *really being there*. It's all too easy to end up in front of the telly all evening. And what about the time spent on phone calls, the newspaper, the hobbies, and the gym or the pub? I've often been amazed at the lack of real contact or conversation between parents and children even when they are all at home each night under the same roof.

**John** (Dad to Pearse, works from home while his wife works abroad):

As a writer I used to find the tension between home life and work life pretty unbearable. Obviously to produce scripts or stories you need to focus pretty intensely and as someone with adult Attention Deficit Disorder I find focusing difficult at the best of times. But try telling that to a little boy who wants help with his homework, a glass of water or just a cuddle.

I agree with Steve that stress is an 'alarm bell' that tells you that something's got to give . . . but if you're hearing the alarm bell don't do like I did and look for the fire in the wrong place. When I first became a parent I wasn't aware that I had ADD (it's a condition normally associated with childhood and, if it doesn't get diagnosed then, it's often missed for years, and sometimes forever). I therefore concluded that the stress and tension I was feeling was because my family insisted on distracting me . . . not because I was naturally predisposed to being distracted!

Unfortunately my way of dealing with this problem – either locking myself away from everyone or disappearing out of the house for long hours to work, morning, noon and night – just created more stress and tension, not to mention missed family occasions and disappointed and lonely family members. (I felt lonely myself on the rare occasions I wasn't working.)

When I did discover I had ADD I had to face the fact that if I was ever going to manage to work effectively I had to plan my work schedule very carefully. Since focus is physically difficult for me I work a lot more effectively by breaking my work periods into shorter more intense bursts, moving onto something else before I get distracted. To my amazement I discovered that I could also fit family time into bouts of work. For instance, instead of leaving the house to work for three hours, I might go to my local café about seven in the evening, write for an hour, come home and spend an hour helping with homework or reading bedtime stories and then pop out again about nine for another hour of work. Or maybe I'll leave the piece of writing aside for the whole evening, play with Pearse and then set the alarm an hour earlier for next morning when I can wake up fresh and get the whole job knocked out in that golden hour before the phone rings or anyone wakes up. In fact, if you've got the leeway of being freelance I have a feeling that working short sharp bursts will allow you to fit in some more family time, whether you've got ADD or not!

## 3. Start pedalling

Do you remember when you first learnt to ride a bike? In theory it seemed like an easy thing to do. After all, if the rest of the kids in the street could do it then there was no reason why you couldn't. But the reality is that struggling to get your balance is never easy for anyone. Things are pretty straightforward while

you are pushing yourself along the kerb or you have the safe hand of an adult holding the back of the seat. The problem is that you are never a real cyclist until you have the courage to start pedalling and venture out on your own. No one ever found their balance before moving off. Only by seizing the moment and starting to pedal do you discover the joy (and the pain) of riding a bike.

Parenting is built on exactly the same principle as riding a bike – it's about getting going and then constantly making little adjustments as you move along. It's about picking yourself off the floor when you lose that all-important balance. It's about learning from your mistakes and having the courage to move on.

Before Corni and I had any children we used to watch some of our friends who had babies or young children and marvel at how stupid they were at being parents. They always seemed to be making glaring errors. We knew that when we became parents we wouldn't fall into the same traps. We would show everyone how parenting should be done. Of course that was nearly twenty years ago now. Back then Corni and I had loads of theories about being parents but no kids. Now we've got loads of kids but no theories.

The experience of being a parent is different for everyone. At the end of the day every parent/child relationship is unique. This means that parenting is about stepping out into the unknown, but if you want the joy (albeit with the associated stress) of bringing up a child, it's a journey you have to take. As a famous phrase of a popular sportswear manufacturer used to proclaim, 'Don't let your fears get in the way of your dreams.' Parenting will never be risk-free. But then the greatest risk in life is not to take any. So get pedalling, and if you start to wobble a little don't get off but simply make some adjustments and keep going.

---

**Daphne** (single mum to James, works full time):

Every situation is so totally different it's difficult not to be swayed by outside forces. There are no standard solutions to this tension between work and family life, so I've had to work it out for myself. Can you ever find a perfect balance? I've had to find out what works for James and me; it may not be perfect and it certainly hasn't been stress-free. For me, being organised has been essential. Once I know the ground rules and work to them I can lead the way for the rest of the family. Being too organised can bring inflexibility and increased tension, so that's a big one to watch for.

Once I'd made a decision about going back to work I wanted to be sure I was 100 per cent confident with the childcare I chose, at least that wouldn't be an area of tension. I took the view that while asking others for their opinion was helpful, who looked after James was ultimately my decision and I had to live with it. For me, that meant a fully qualified nanny, living in.

---

Feelings of guilt, worry and anxiety are all natural; I've found it helpful to take a fresh look at the tension and thrive on it. I'm particularly bad at being realistic about what I can take on, which has put extra, unnecessary pressure on me at times. Constantly thinking I have to be 'doing' can be exhausting for me as well as those around me! Just 'being' is often more than acceptable – especially to a teenage boy.

As James grows older, the tension between my work and home life changes. Listening to what's going on in his head as he moves through adolescence becomes more of a challenge and less easy to discern. That takes time. Am I prepared or able to make that time? I'd like to think so.

## 4. Be prepared to make mistakes, but pursue excellence

Success as a working parent isn't about being a perfect working parent. That's impossible. It's not our failures as parents that get in the way of our success but simply how we choose to respond to them. Only by facing up to the areas in which we are weak and tackling them head-on will we learn and move on. In truth, no parent ever loses their L-plates but nor should they give up on their driving lessons.

When Michael Jackson spoke at the Oxford Student Union he openly stated in front of the students and the world's press, 'I am the product of my childhood.' The man who the media likes to portray as 'Wacko Jacko' was laying his troubles and behaviour as an adult right at the door of his parents. And it's not just the rich and famous who claim that their problems stem from poor parenting. A personal and troubled friend of mine is convinced that he's still basically a 'prisoner of his childhood'. Some would argue that it's enough to put anyone off ever wanting to become a parent. But while it's true that the way a parent behaves today has a fundamental impact on what their child will become tomorrow, the reality is that the majority of children do grow to be well-adjusted adults. The truth is, if you are willing and courageous enough to take some time to address the problems we all face as parents, rather than attempting to 'do an ostrich' – burying your head in the sand and hoping they disappear – then you will do a great job. Parenting is not Mission Impossible, but it will keep you on your toes.

---

**Andy and Debbie** (Mum and Dad to Sam – Andy works from home, Debbie is a part-time nurse)

**Debbie**: I know that my job has taken second place because I don't have the desire to go the second mile by bringing work home with me, because I know I have commitments the minute I leave my workplace. This is frustrating for me as I've always been someone who is keen and committed to my work and likes to get new ideas off the ground quickly by putting in extra time and effort. I have had to let go of a lot of this but realise in the future I will be able to be more committed to work when Sam is older. Samuel is now my priority and my career will have to remain on hold for the time being. Many opportunities have arisen for my promotion, which I have turned down because I feel I would not be able to give the commitment required. As everyone keeps telling me (even people at work), your children are only young once and so should be enjoyed while you can.

The wonderful thing about Andy working from home is that if Sam is poorly and cannot go to nursery he can look after him, which may mean rescheduling his workload but enables me not to let my workplace down, which would affect the care of the sick children I'm responsible for. Even though I cannot commit to my job outside of my working hours I am determined to give it 100 per cent while I am there and it is important that I do not let the hospital down as a result of being forced to stay at home with Samuel. Andy and I discussed this before I agreed to return to work and he was happy to take on this responsibility as and when required.

**Andy**: I have Samuel one day a week and when work is steady it's not a problem but when there are tight deadlines things can get a little stressed. Debbie often gets frustrated when she returns home to find the washing up not done and the rubbish not taken out, as a result of me having taken the opportunity to work while Sam's been asleep. I also used to enjoy playing football regularly at the weekend, but soon realised that this activity needed to be reduced so that Debs wasn't left with Sam on her own every Saturday.

## 5. Learn to see the funny side

Why did the crab go to prison? Because he kept pinching things. OK, so perhaps it's not the greatest joke in the world, but to the four-year-old who told it, it was a real side-splitter that soon had his dad giggling along with him.

Sadly, being a parent isn't always as funny, and the stresses and strains can really take their toll. In some cases it can taint the whole way we look at day-to-day life, extracting all the joy from it. So many of the daily niggles of balancing work with home life may seem trivial on their own, but put them all together and even the most even-tempered of us can begin to feel the strain. Laughter can prevent tense relationships getting out of hand, boosts morale in tough times and keeps life in perspective. It's also proven that laughing helps to lower our blood pressure, reduce levels of stress hormones and boost the immune system. That's why it's so important to reflect on events that have added to the tension and begin to see their funny side.

Laughter also has the added advantage of bringing people closer together. Most families have plenty of material for shared jokes, be it Dad's fashion sense, a disastrous day out, or the birthday party you'll never forget.

A couple of years ago my children planned to make me breakfast on my birthday. However, knowing that I had to leave the house at 7 a.m. sharp, they arranged for this to take place nice and early – very early! In fact they were so keen to celebrate that they all put on their alarms for 5 a.m. Unfortunately, these proved to be just that bit too early and, as a result, they all fell back to sleep, if indeed they ever woke up in the first place. This had a decidedly bad impact on the start of my birthday celebrations – because it was already 6.30 by the time we all finally woke up. The kids were upset, the breakfast was not made and what should have been a leisurely and fun present-opening session instantly became a very stressful, tense and tearful twenty-five minutes as my deadline loomed.

However, as we crowded round the kitchen table ferociously munching cereal, and I ripped open my presents, Friday (our cat) ran into the room and began sniffing around excitedly. He often does strange things, so we didn't take much notice until he suddenly sprang into action. A mouse darted out from under the table and ran full-pelt across the floor. Friday pounced. But no sooner had he caught it in his mouth than Corni, my wife, and several of the children simultaneously let out a deafening shriek. Friday was so startled by this that he dropped the mouse, which then scuttled to safety behind a large cupboard. For the next twenty minutes, until I had to leave, Friday and half of the family tried – and failed – to recapture the mouse, while the other half stood on chairs, as paralysed by fear of the mouse as no doubt it was of them.

We could easily have chosen to see that morning as a disaster. But the truth is, even though I've forgotten most, if not all, of the presents I received that day, none of us will ever forget that birthday breakfast. It may not have worked out the way we had envisaged it, but years from now we'll laugh about the 'year of the rodent' and have fond memories because we experienced it together.

**Stewart and Angela** (Angela is at home full time, they have four children, two from Angela's previous relationship)

**Angela**: Organisation is not my strong point, and getting the children organised is definitely one of my poor qualities. I remember it was awful having four children at four different schools. James was at our Catholic senior school, Naomi was at a school for children with moderate learning disabilities, Denise was at a school for physically disabled children and Nessie was at our local primary school. I remember I always had four different letters sent home and four different times when they got home. I remember having to juggle everything and think, 'What time do we all have to be at home by?' These tensions were very hard at first.

Stewart used to say to me a lot, 'My mum had to cope with two children and she never had an untidy home.' I've learnt, though, that housework isn't the most important thing, and can be put on the back burner if it means I can do extra homework with Nessie. I've learnt that I make mistakes as a mum and as a wife but my children still love me just the same.

Laughter is important – we laugh a lot. We've been in our new house nearly four years and we've only just painted the front room. We've learnt to sit down, light a candle and listen to music. Sometimes I have a bath to release the tension. When tension is bad I always have a headache. I know I must sit back and hopefully relax just for five minutes or so.

## Remember

- No working parent has the balance perfectly right – it's a continual process of making small adjustments.
- Being a parent is a steep learning curve, so mistakes are inevitable.
- Stress is your friend – it's an in-built defence system that prompts you to take action.
- Feeling the tension does not mean you are failing, it means that you are concerned for the welfare of your children.
- Spontaneity often takes a bit of organisation.
- Being around the house isn't the same as really *being there* for your child.

## Key principle

**You can't get rid of the tension completely, but you can turn it into something positive.**

## How to achieve it

- Listen to the warning bells of stress from yourself and those around you, and take immediate action to reduce its impact.
- Organise your home life with the attention that you use to organise your work life.
- Don't be afraid to experiment a little in order to discover what works for you and your family.
- Don't dwell on your mistakes – learn from them and move on.
- Be courageous – willing to address the problems you face as a parent.
- Learn to see the funny side, even in difficult situations.

# Deal with Guilt

---

**WANTED: AN INDIVIDUAL WITH A FLAIR FOR:**

| | |
|---|---|
| Lion Taming | Plate Spinning |
| Juggling | Tightrope Walking |
| Acrobatics | Clowning |

Applications in writing to **PARENTS-R-US plc.**

---

One day, Doug decided that having a few other 'Dougs' around would make life a little easier. So he started experimenting with cloning. Before long there were several Dougs, all suited to the various aspects of his life. One was an expert in housework and looking after the children, one took his place at work, which left the original Doug with time on his hands to do whatever he chose.

Every parent must, at one time or another, have dreamt about what it would be like to have a clone or two to help out with life's ceaseless demands. Wouldn't it be great to be able to be in four places at once? You could put in a full day at the office, get all the housework done, drop the kids off at school, pick them up, take them swimming, cook them an evening meal, put them to bed, read to them for half an hour each and still have plenty of time for 'yourself' – a parenting paradise.

Back in the real world, the trouble is that there *is* only one of us, spread all too thinly over the competing demands that are made on us. Unlike Doug, from the film *Multiplicity*, we just *can't* be in more than one place at a time. And as a result it's all

too easy to end up crippled by emotional guilt. Guilt that we're not there for our child when we should be, guilt that we are neglecting our partner, guilt that we are not giving all that we can to our employer. And on top of all that, we feel a deep frustration that we are not really even there for ourselves.

Mike is a father of four and over the last eight years he's been running his own business. Reflecting on the demands placed upon him, Mike observed, 'The problem is that I'm responsible for my family and responsible for my staff. It's a huge pressure. I feel it's all down to me. I started off on my own but now the company has grown, I'm all too aware that it's my contacts who put the food on the plates of my employees' families, as well as my own. We just can't afford to lose any clients and that means I have to put the hours in. I try to draw a definite line between work and home. The way I handle it is that I would rather stay late at the office to do what needs to be done than bring work home and end up shutting myself away from the family. This balancing act is great when it works, but when it gets out of control on either side I really start to feel the pressure. When I'm too busy with work I feel guilty that it's my wife who ends up doing all the parenting duties, but at the same time I know that I'm only trying to keep the business going. When I get absorbed in home life I feel guilty that I'm leaving too much for my colleagues to cope with without my leadership. Either way I can't win. I'm damned if I do and damned if I don't. There doesn't seem to be any way out.'

Is Mike right? Do you just have to grin and bear it? Or are there things you can do which will make a difference? Here are four principles to get you thinking:

## 1. Ask yourself why you feel guilty

There are two kinds of guilt: the kind that's legitimate and the kind that's illegitimate. To succeed as a working parent it's vital that you learn to tell the difference. Legitimate guilt can be a real friend, alerting you to issues you need to face up to and deal with – never try to squash it or ignore it. Instead face up to the issue and deal with it. But what many of us suffer from a lot of the time is the other, vague, nebulous, nagging feeling that we can't ever really pin down but that slowly pulls us down all the same.

Imagine yourself driving home one evening after a long day at work. As you do so, a police car suddenly pulls out behind you and starts to follow you. You're not speeding; you're driving with due care and attention; all your lights are working and you've not been drinking. In fact you are sure that you've done nothing wrong. Yet somehow you still feel guilty. You know it's stupid but you can't help it. *That's* illegitimate guilt. It's part of the human psyche, but it's misplaced and totally irrational.

Legitimate guilt, on the other hand, speaks for itself. This time you are driving home, but you are late and in a hurry – your speed is over the legal limit, you're being careless and you know it. When the police car pulls out behind you, you know that you're guilty and there's no getting away from it.

The problem with the struggle to maintain work/life balance is that, in much the same way, our feelings of guilt are sometimes legitimate and sometimes illegitimate, and it's very easy to end up confused. Our feelings are not necessarily a good or accurate guide to steer by. We end up feeling guilty about things we have no control over as well as those we do.

DO YOU EVER FEEL GUILTY ABOUT BEING A WORKING PARENT?

NO... AND THAT'S JUST ONE MORE THING I BEAT MYSELF UP ABOUT!!

For instance, many working parents with a child of pre-school age need to work, and use some form of childcare provision in the form of a relative or family friend, a day school or even a crèche provided by their company. The fact remains that however appropriate and well organised it is, and even though they know that their child will have a great time with the other children and that if they didn't work the child would miss out in lots of other ways, when it comes to being away from them, they still somehow end up feeling guilty.

---

**Daphne** (single mum to James, works full time):

If I'm really honest, guilt about working hasn't been a big issue for me. I was more likely to feel guilty for not carrying a photo of James with me than whether I worked or not. That's probably because there wasn't really a choice – about work. In the early days I was too busy handling life to feel guilty. But with the work/home tension that builds up, comes guilt. I've found that a degree of guilt can prod me in to positive action. When I'm feeling a failure of a parent, who's out of the house for at least twelve hours a day, I give myself a reality check. Is James a fun guy to be with? Yes! Is he enjoying school and living a healthy social life? Yes! Am I fulfilled in a job that pays the bills? Mostly! I've had to learn to be extremely honest with myself and try to learn from my mistakes.

'Does James know that you're his mum?' It's a simple question to a working parent with a full-time, live-in nanny, the sort of question that can inspire enormous feelings of guilt. But I'd decided what suited us both and had to live with it. What's more, I know the truth. The truth is that there has never been any doubt as to who is James' mum. Me!

By no stretch of the imagination am I a clock-watcher at work but on the odd occasion when I've had to leave a meeting on time or decline an invitation to an after-work drink I have felt incredibly guilty. There's never been any 'tutting' but I almost see eyes rolling. I'm still learning to ignore those moments!

---

> The one person who has never made me feel guilty is James. I have always been honest with him. He understands the reality of life and, whatever else they are, children are very forgiving. Between us we have been able to turn any negatives into positives and start again.

No matter how conscientious you are as a parent there are going to be times when choices will have to be made that will leave you with that gnawing sense of guilt that is often illegitimate or misplaced. So when you do feel guilty, take the time to sit down, think through your feelings and try honestly to analyse why you feel guilty about a particular situation. Are those feelings legitimate or not? And because it's difficult to understand and analyse your own feelings it often helps to talk things through with a friend that you trust as well – there's nothing like an objective opinion to liberate you. On the other hand, if you decide that the guilt you feel is legitimate and justified, it should provide you with the motivation to do something about it and make some changes. Of course, even if you do decide that the guilt you feel isn't justified, you may still *feel* guilty. It's natural, normal and healthy to be concerned about your child – being a parent at the best of times is a rollercoaster experience – but it's also vital to keep things in perspective, concentrating your energy on the things you can change and should deal with, while having the confidence to learn not to be crippled by those things you can't change.

In the film *Liar, Liar*, Jim Carey plays a divorcee who is always making promises to spend time with his boy, which he invariably fails to keep. As the guilt of his failure to keep his word becomes ever greater he resorts to spending hours on the phone to his son coming up with even 'bigger and better' ideas for things they *will* do together. But true to form he fails to fulfil these because of his work commitments and priorities. And when he fails to deliver he resorts to buying endless presents coupled with even bigger and emptier promises of what they will do next weekend . . . next holiday . . . next birthday. In the end, his utterly frustrated son makes a birthday wish that just for one day his dad would not be able to lie. That way, if he wasn't planning to be around then at least he would have to be honest about it. Children value your honesty and love much more than empty promises or gifts.

We naturally want to do the best for our kids. But our enthusiasm can often get the better of us and lead us to make unrealistic promises that we find impossible to keep. It would be great to be there for our children 24/7 but we live in the real world. It's far better to be realistic with yourself and honest with your child. That way you can keep the promises you do make, get rid of the main causes of real guilt and build a much stronger relationship of trust with your child.

---

**John** (Dad to Pearse, works from home while his wife works abroad):

When my wife moved away to work overseas I had serious guilt on two levels. In the first place I felt guilty that I wasn't earning enough to make it possible for her to stay at home. Guilt is of course a master of deception – in actual fact my wife is one of the most talented business people I've ever met. She'd spotted an overseas opportunity and decided to go for it and is now so successful she's got a chain of stores both overseas and at home. There's nothing wrong with being a stay-at-home partner of course, it's just that now with the benefit of hindsight we both realise it was never going to be right for Mrs Byrne.

The second level of guilt was on our son's behalf because he didn't have both parents around all the time. Again, guilt was interfering with my perception. For starters his mum certainly hadn't abandoned him – we remain in constant contact while she is away

---

and when she is home on buying trips she takes over the parenting reins. My large family of in-laws are also always on hand to help out with baby-sitting and parenting chores.

I guess what I was really feeling guilty about was my own lack of experience and organisational skills as a parent, and I 'coped' with this guilt by buying far too many sweets and toys and basically by spoiling my son rotten. One day someone pointed out that I was actually overcompensating for the lack of a 'nuclear family' environment that I'd grown up in, but which my son had never actually known. If you don't know something you can't miss it.

Now instead of trying to recapture my own childhood memories I concentrate on creating good memories of our family for my son to cherish in the future. And that involves time and planning, not sweets!

## 2. Learn from your mistakes

Good decisions are the result of wisdom. Wisdom is the result of experience. Experience is the result of bad decisions. Failure isn't making mistakes – we all do that. Failure is what happens when you give up rather than learning from the bad decisions of your past and moving on. Rather than beating ourselves up about our errors of judgement, and short-sightedness in balancing home and work, your needs and your child's needs, it's much better to adopt an attitude that views even big mistakes as 'springboards' to getting it right next time around. Life is one big learning curve – even the biggest mistakes provide an opportunity to learn and move on.

The truth is, there's no sure-fire way to raise a perfect and happy child. And there's no magic formula, $\Sigma=mc^2$, that'll give you instant success as a working parent. There's not even any guarantee that what worked with your first child will work with your second, third or even fourth – and I speak from experience! Parenting isn't an exact science. There are no foolproof, money-back, guaranteed, universally applicable methods for achieving your desired end result.

If being a parent is life's greatest adventure, it's also its greatest experiment. A lot of the time it comes down to trial and error: unplannable, unpredictable and chaotic. Even having lots of children doesn't qualify someone to dispense absolute, set-in-stone, tried and tested, Good Housekeeping Seal of Approval rules for success – because there just aren't any! Other parents can share what they've learnt from personal experience but no one can give you fail-safe, guaranteed-to-succeed rules for what to do in every situation, because your experience as a working parent is unique. And what's more, as your child grows they are constantly changing, so even when you've been at it for years, you still have to make most of it up as you go along, adapting what you've learned to suit today's situation. Parenting is rather like playing jazz; there are some signposts to follow, a basic chord structure that will see you through to the end, but mostly it's about improvisation, doing what you feel works best. You are bound to play some bum chords along the way but the band's still playing and the show must go on.

What's more, however long you've been at it, you'll still get frustrated with your own performance. Books, courses and good friends can help a lot, but whatever you've heard or read, you still won't ever get it all right. Don't torture yourself with

DO YOU GET MUCH TIME FOR FAMILY HOLIDAYS?

NO... BUT I GO ON FREQUENT GUILT TRIPS.

unrealistic expectations of doing a 'perfect' job – which just isn't possible for *anyone*. Instead, try to relax and enjoy being a parent.

---

**Catherine and Paul** (married with three children – Paul works full time, Catherine is on a career break)

**Catherine**: We've found that it's often other people's views and comments that make you feel worse or even make you feel guilty when there's really no need to. When I returned to work after Luke was born, we didn't really feel guilty at all. I had to go back to work because we needed the money and I was desperate for the stimulation of work.

We had a great nanny and I was completely confident that Luke was stimulated and cared for while I was at work. I loved my job and, once I got home, our evenings and weekends were completely and willingly devoted to our baby.

What made me feel guilty were comments from others, such as, 'He's such a beautiful baby – do you find it hard leaving him?' or, roughly translated, 'Don't you love your baby? You should be at home with him!' Backed up by Paul, I would immediately get on the defensive and retort with all the excuses I could think of – now I realise we had no reason to feel guilty.

We were in for a heavy dose of guilt after Grace, our daughter, was born. We moved, taking on a bigger house, and I went back to work when she was five months old. Our plans to be settled into the new house before my return to work went wrong and we ended up moving just one week beforehand and a few days after our nanny started. There was lots of essential work to be done on the house so, basically, I 'swanned' off to work, leaving the children (three years and five months respectively) with nanny on a 'building site'. It was awful – I am still amazed that she didn't leave.

During that period, I was so stressed most of the time that both my family and work suffered. After such a horrible start, things did settle down – the children and nanny were fine and the house was put back together again.

---

Even when I started working part time and my son went to nursery then school, I found a new reason for guilt. I wanted to show an interest in the school but found that so many events (meetings, impromptu singing/poetry), seemed to happen on the days I was at work – more guilt! I scoured the school newsletter with a fine-toothed comb for advance warning of things I could arrange to be at. We also pleaded with the head teacher for more notice of events for us poor 'guilt-ridden' working parents – it all helped.

Then there were those 'very annoying mums' who helped in the classroom, contributing their creative gifts – of which I felt I had none. Eventually I started helping in Luke's reception class on my day off, while Grace was at nursery. It felt like I was making up for all the times I hadn't been there. Luke loved having me at school and I loved every minute of it too, discovering a speck of creativity I didn't know I had!

Now I'm at home I still feel guilty, just about different things like not home-cooking enough – they still get chicken nuggets and chips regularly – or looking forward to the day our toddler goes to the nursery – the same old guilt.

The only way we deal with all this is to try not to dwell on guilt but to focus on the positive – show your children (and partner) lots of love and try to set up the best working arrangement for your family, the best childcare that you can afford and hours that, if possible, suit your family life. We also found that admitting our guilty feelings to each other and others really helps – we can help each other and talk through solutions. A guilt shared is a guilt halved.

## 3. Turn your guilty feelings into positive action

C. S. Lewis, the author of the Narnia chronicles, famously stated, 'Love anything and your heart will be torn.' Lewis knew more than anyone that to love is to risk pain and heartache. Love brings us enormous joy but it also makes us vulnerable to the pain of life, the price you have to pay for commitment to other people in relationships. It's therefore no surprise that, from time to time, being a parent can be a painful experience – love hurts. But the pain can also be a learning experience that reveals issues that need dealing with in order to maintain a healthy relationship.

As we've learnt already, feeling guilty doesn't mean you're a bad parent, in fact it is more likely to be a sign of the love you have for your child. But it's also a reasonable indicator that you could be a better parent. Talking to friends, your family, perhaps even reading this book might just challenge you about creative ways in which you can balance your work with your home life. But at the end of the day, one of the greatest motivators to change is the way you feel about your relationship with your child. If your own emotions are telling you that your work has been taking you away from your child for more time than is healthy then resolve to do something about it. Once you've been able to work out whether those niggling feelings of guilt are trying to tell you something, it is often pretty clear what you need to do to change things. If, however, it's not clear, at least you are on the pathway to beginning to think through your options. And don't forget that one of the best things that can come out of even the toughest of these situations is the opportunity to apologise to your child and to ask them to forgive you for the mistakes you have made, which, of course, is never a sign of weakness but rather of strength and the fact that you want to keep your relationship with your child healthy.

---

**Stewart and Angela** (Angela is at home full time, they have four children, two from Angela's previous relationship)

**Angela**: Stewart and I always thought that it should be Stewart who went out to work and it was my job to be at home. We decided that when we got married because I was already at home looking after Naomi and James. I tried looking after Naomi and

James and working when I was on my own. I felt guilty for leaving them with my parents, who were still alive then. Everyone asked me, 'How can you leave them?', and with all Naomi's problems I kept having to take time off. I wasn't getting home till late and I felt it wasn't good for them.

Stewart work shifts so he does sometimes feel guilty when he cannot be with them for special activities. He always wants to know how things went; sometimes Nessie stays up to tell him about it. We felt it was right for me to be at home, and Stewart is happy doing what he does.

The girls always say to Stewart, 'You've got to go out to work so Mummy can spend the money – with our help!' Nessie, the youngest, always asks if she can go to work with him! When he was a bus conductor she sometimes went out with him on the bus, she enjoyed it so much. It meant that they spent time together and it helped Stewart not to feel guilty for not being there all the time. Shift work does help, sometimes Stewart can be there when the kids come home from school.

## 4. Remember that your child wants to forgive you

Finally, it's always a great relief for parents to discover a fundamental truth about children – however wrong things have gone, deep down they will want to put them straight. In our failure they still love us, just as we continue to love them when they fail and let us down. Children have an in-built desire to make their relationship with their parents work. What they are looking for isn't a perfect parent but one who is obviously trying to do their best – and that's what they will remember and appreciate as they get older and become parents themselves.

A friend of mine used to get really hung up about whether he had been a success as a dad. He wrestled constantly with all the occasions he could recall of his failure to keep promises, the times he had let his children down or failed, in his eyes, to be the perfect dad. Eventually the agony became too much and so he decided to risk asking his five children for feedback about how they felt he had done and was doing as their father. To his surprise and great relief there wasn't a single negative comment from them, and no spotlight was shone anywhere near the mountain of failures he had perceived. In his own words, 'Not one of my children mentioned my excessive discipline, over-commitment to work, my negativity when they needed and deserved praise or my tendency to jump to wrong conclusions.' The reality was, as is the case with most children, that they had forgiven their dad his failings because they could see that he was constantly doing his best for them. Their memories were of a dad who was there for them, supporting them, spending time with them, being spontaneous and demonstrating his love to them.

The knowledge that your child is very forgiving should never be used as an excuse not to work at your relationship with them, or as a licence for complacency or selfishness, but so that even when we blow it we know there is always a way forward. All parents are free to fail. So accept forgiveness from those you need to and move on – tomorrow, as they say, is another day.

---

**Andy and Debbie**: (Mum and Dad to Sam – Andy works from home, Debbie is a part-time nurse)

**Debbie**: After ten months of being Mummy it was really, really hard to accept that someone else was required to look after Sam. We even considered moving house to be nearer family but this was not appropriate at that time. I had chosen to return to work after maternity leave but was unprepared for the guilt that ensued. I was able to negotiate that I only went back for two days a week because I felt that this was all I could bear. I needed to trust others to look after him, which I had found hard from the very day I had him – I even found it hard to leave him with baby-sitters. I could not take

---

Samuel to nursery for the first few months because I didn't want the trauma of leaving him so Andy took him instead. Going back to work was enough for me to cope with. It took a good few months for me to realise that not only was Samuel OK but he actually really enjoyed nursery and often didn't want to leave at the end of the day.

He is now almost two and he still cries for five minutes when he is left at the beginning of the day at nursery but is always happy when we collect him.

I know that often children who start nursery before the age of one settle in better than older children. Also some children don't like it and don't ever really settle into the nursery environment. Happily Samuel is a child who suits nursery life but I would not want to send him more than two days a week because I want us to have the most influence on his life at this early age.

## Remember

- The real world isn't the ideal world, so even the most conscientious parent will have times when they feel guilty.
- There are two kinds of guilt: illegitimate – about things that you actually have little control over; and legitimate – about things you can change.
- It's natural, normal and healthy to be concerned about the welfare of your child.
- Failure isn't making mistakes. Rather, it is giving up instead of learning from the errors we make.
- It may take some time but, fundamentally, your child wants to forgive you for the times when you've got it wrong.

## Key principle

**Turn any legitimate feelings of guilt into positive action – don't just let them fester by doing nothing.**

## How to achieve it

- Don't ignore feelings of guilt – face up to the issue and deal with it.
- Think through your feelings and honestly analyse why you feel guilty.
- Keep things in perspective and focus on the things you can change. Don't be crippled by those you can't.
- Use mistakes as 'springboards' to getting it right next time.
- Be realistic with yourself and honest with your child – apologise for times when you have got your priorities wrong.
- Ask for and accept forgiveness from those you need to and move on.
- Talk to family and friends about getting the balance right.

**Part Two**

# Taking Control

# Budget Carefully

'Never invest money in anything that needs to eat', once said a famous financier. Interesting, perhaps even useful, advice. But even if it's true, it's too late for you!

As every parent knows, children take a great deal of financial investment. Not only do they consume food quicker than you can say 'McDonald's Corporation', but by the time your child is old enough to be earning a wage of their own you will have spent tens of thousands of pounds on nappies, pushchairs, clothing, shoes, toys, games, childcare, hobbies, parties, bikes, pocket money, computers, holidays, education, dentist bills and healthcare – and that's just for starters. While the cost of a child should never be a reason not to have one, there's no harm in remembering that children don't come cheap.

If money is of no concern to you, you might want to skip this chapter. However, in truth, the majority of working parents are earning a wage primarily in order to make ends meet. But more than that, while most of us know how much we earn it's surprising how few of us have a real grip on where that money is going and how much life is really costing us. In fact, government research shows that the majority of families significantly underestimate the amount of debt they are really in, with the true figure, in some cases, being ten times the figure *guessed* by the parents.

**Catherine and Paul** (married with three children – Paul works full time, Catherine is on a career break)

**Catherine**: Before we had children, budgeting was fairly straightforward and with both of us working full time in reasonably paid jobs, it was never a big issue. We naively went into parenting thinking things wouldn't change much. It didn't take us long to realise that financially, as well as in every other way, life would never be quite the same again.

When I went back to work first time after an extended maternity leave, we hadn't really planned ahead at all – after ten months we found ourselves suddenly broke and I was panicked into going back to work full time. We started looking for a nanny, and soon discovered that even this cost money we didn't have – advertisements and agency fees – quite apart from the wages we'd have to pay to get the person we wanted. With hindsight, we were so laid back (some would say irresponsible) and completely absorbed in our new family life that I think we were in another world. On top of this we also had to find money for my work clothes and season ticket – it was a pretty lean time!

We just about got through, and were more prepared second time around. I again took some unpaid maternity leave even though we had just moved and had all the costs of that to bear. We budgeted in advance and got used to taking a calculator round Tesco's, putting things back when we went over our limit. I wasn't able to afford lunch in the staff canteen for the first few weeks after my return. Paying the nanny was the priority, eating came second!

When Paul was promoted we considered the possibility of me working fewer hours. We felt everyone would benefit from me going part time, thought seriously about the financial implications on the family and did our figures properly. It seemed quite tight but, although we did not have so much money, we also saved (a little) on childcare and travelling costs. Other expenses, however, like work clothes and eating out (lunches, leaving dos, team nights out, etc.) remained the same – it's easy to forget this. In the end our budgeting was worth it and we actually found ourselves better off than we'd thought!

While thinking about a third child we considered how this would affect us financially. We knew that if I went back to work childcare for three would be at best expensive and at worst unworkable. We were fortunate to be in a position where I had a choice as we could exist on just Paul's salary. I still opted to give working a go and reduced my hours to two days a week – which still paid off financially – just.

I'm glad I went back to work (it proved I was still capable!), but six months afterwards we decided it was time for a change. I was offered a career break for two years (unpaid) with the option of returning to a similar position, an offer that seemed too good to refuse.

We were slow in getting organised about budgeting – I don't know how we got away with it for so long. Now we realise that the financial implications of decisions you make are vital – if you get it wrong, it can be a source of tension for both partners that can so easily be avoided.

We'd urge anyone thinking of changing their working hours or taking time out to plan ahead financially and save in advance to prepare for this if possible – we didn't! Also make sure you're fully aware about how the changes may affect benefits or your pension – it can all make a lot of difference.

The thought of an evening spent poring over your domestic finances is hardly everyone's (anyone's?) idea of fun. Checks and balances, coupled with the prospect of a dawning reality that we have less money than we thought we did, is unlikely to feature high on your list of 'Things I'd love to do if I had a few hours to spare'. The truth of the matter, however, is that if you really want to seize your own work/life balance by the scruff of the neck, making a realistic assessment of where you currently stand financially is an essential first step. Having an accurate grasp of your financial position is a key to solving the jigsaw because, once you know where you are, you'll be better able to make judgements about the options that are open to you. Without thorough knowledge of your financial situation you will find it nearly impossible to make an informed decision about whether you need to work full time, part time or not at all, let alone which childcare options you can afford. The good news, however, is that even the most basic of budgets will yield some remarkable insights into your spending habits and how much 'unallocated' money you really have to spend. It shouldn't take long to put a budget together, but the payoff will be both immediate and tangible.

Having even a simple budget is a good idea because:

- *It helps you to know what is going on.* Ignorance may be bliss in the eyes of some, but when it comes to your finances you just can't afford to bury your head in the sand. A simple budget will soon tell you what money you have and, more importantly, what money you don't have.
- *It helps you take charge.* Though facing up to the positives and the negatives of your financial situation might seem daunting, in fact it is likely to be very liberating, as it will give you the information you need to take control of your finances instead of feeling that they are controlling you.
- *It helps you communicate.* If you share your income with your partner, budgeting will help avoid the tensions that can so easily emerge as a result of personal differences over how to handle your finances and prioritise spending.
- *It helps you spot potential problems.* There are enough surprises to cope with as a parent without letting your finances become another one. Though you will always have unforeseen expenses, by keeping close control of your financial situation, you will be better equipped to cope when they do arise. Planning ahead may even reduce the number of nasty little surprises.
- *It helps you save time in the long run.* A stitch in time saves

nine. Having financial control doesn't mean spending loads of time on paperwork each month. A few hours used well to set your budgeting system up in the first place will create a good foundation, which will then only require a little time each month to keep up to date. And on top of that, it will have the added bonus of saving you the time and energy you spend panicking and worrying over your finances.

- *It helps you save money in the long run.* Having a budget need not mean that you are destined to lead a life of penny-pinching frugality. In fact, by taking better control of your finances, and being aware of your income and outgoings, you may well find ways of saving money and so end up with a little extra for the occasional frivolous spending spree, or a little less time at work and a little more time at home!

---

**John** (Dad to Pearse, works from home while his wife works abroad):

I've already mentioned from my own experience how my first response in the face of parental guilt was to throw money at the problem. Bigger toys, more sweets, etc. I think I first saw the error of my ways a couple of Christmasses ago when I bought my son one of those groundbreaking, expensive robotic dogs. I think the most groundbreaking thing about it was that of any Christmas toy it had the shortest shelf-life I have ever seen. It wasn't that he broke it ... I think I would have preferred even that ... it's that after Robodog had run through his selection of tricks about twice, Pearse was completely bored with it. Mind you, my own life got a bit more exciting in January when the toy shop's storecard bill arrived. Doing some quick budget analysis helped me see that in my own head I was equating being a good parent with how much money I spent.

What that Christmas morning showed me was that my son wasn't assessing things on the same criteria as I was – he judges

---

my parenting on the time I spend with him, not the money. So, if one of my excuses for working so much is so I can earn money to have time to spend with my kid, why don't I just save a little money instead of spending on stuff we don't need? I can then afford to work a little less and spend the time saved with my family – which is what I was supposed to be working for in the first place. Wow! Maths so simple even I can understand it!

(By the way, a by-product of my learning better money habits has been developing the confidence to model better financial management for Pearse... Dumb Toy Stores of the Next Generation, be very, very afraid.)

## How do I do it?

The place to start working out your budget is to be sure of your net income (the amount you have left after your employer has taken tax, national insurance, your pension and any other deductions out of your wages). For many people this will be in the form of a salary paid directly into their bank account each month. However, you may be paid weekly or through a pay packet in cash. However you are paid, the important thing is to know exactly how much you earn as well as the day or date on which you normally receive your wages. Now you have to decide whether you are going to budget on a weekly or monthly basis. The simplest option is to base your budget on the period for which your employer pays you each time you receive your salary.

Assuming you opt for a month-by-month budget, follow these five steps:

## 1. Monitor everything you spend for a month

Buy yourself a small notepad and carry it with you all the time for an entire month. Write down a list of everything that you spend money on during that month. And that means everything

– from petrol to groceries, magazines to dog food, parking meters to pints down the pub. It's a complete pain, but it's a one-off and is guaranteed to surprise as well as inform you! You may find the temptation of a cup of coffee and a bacon sandwich every morning all too hard to resist, but once you see how much you're spending on it, you may find yourself starting to think a bit differently. (Just a bacon sandwich every *other* day, perhaps.)

## 2. Work out your monthly expenditure

Now, using the list you have compiled, categorise what you spend (food, petrol or travel, clothes, treats, going out, cigarettes, etc.). You will need to include things such as rent or mortgage, house insurance, phone bills, utilities (gas, water, electricity), council tax, credit card bills, car payments, TV licence, student loans and any other direct debits or standing orders that go out of your account each month, plus money put aside for holidays, savings, etc. A careful scan down your bank statement will soon give you a clear idea what these headings should be. Lastly, make a 'guesstimate' of what you should allow for unforeseen or unexpected expenditure – what if the car needs a new tyre, etc.? Now, using your 'average' month's list as a guide, write out your regular monthly expenditure.

A word of warning here: Just about everyone is offering the 'ease' of paying for those 'necessities' by monthly direct debit these days. But though these schemes can help to spread out the cost of expensive items to make them more manageable, at the same time it's all too easy to fall into the trap of signing up for things you really can't afford. Remind yourself that they *will* have to be paid for in the end.

## 3. Work out your monthly income

Not all your income will come from your salary or wages. You should also take into account family allowance or other benefits you may be receiving, as well as interest on any savings you may have. Once you are sure you have listed everything that brings in money add it up to establish your monthly income.

## 4. Work out your monthly balance

Be warned, comparing your income with your expenditure may result in quite a shock. But if you do find that you are spending more than you're getting in, it's time to make some urgent changes (and that doesn't mean extending your overdraft or the credit limit on your Mastercard). Think through the expenditure that you actually need (or really want) and be honest about what you could save on or do without. Inevitably there will have to be some soul-searching. Do you really need eighty TV channels with nothing on being piped into your home? What about only buying a weekend newspaper with a news-review section rather than spending money on a daily? As the saying goes, 'Look after the pennies and the pounds will look after themselves.' I'm not suggesting that you should cut out all of life's little luxuries, but simply engage in an honest appraisal of the amount of money you are spending on a month to month basis.

## 5. Continue to keep an eye on income and outgoings

It's never pleasurable to have to keep an eye on your finances, but in the long run it is bound to help you use your money more wisely and will slowly help you into a stronger financial position than you may have otherwise thought possible. The good news is that most of the hard work will be over within the first month or two. Then it's simply a matter of monitoring how it's going month by month, to make sure that things aren't getting out of hand and that you are taking into account any major changes such as a pay rise, a drop in salary, a rent increase or a change in your mortgage rate, etc.

**Angela and Stewart** (Angela is at home full time, they have four children, two from Angela's previous relationship)

**Angela**: As a couple we decided that it was best for Stewart to do all the budgeting on the computer. When James was a baby I went back to work so money was not a problem until I gave up working. We have decided to save over the next few months so that we can have a holiday with the children, as this year we did not have a family holiday. Benefit can help but we have to remember that it is not always for good, sometimes you have to reapply and that takes time.

Stewart has decided to have a rest day when he doesn't work. He could earn more money but if he did that he would not see the kids as much.

## Two more hints

First, work hard to pay off your debts. But never fall into the trap of borrowing more money to do so. If you think that you may be in trouble with debt, don't put off admitting it for one more day. You are not alone; there are billions of pounds outstanding in the UK on credit and storecards alone. In fact it's estimated that one third of all families experience serious financial problems at some stage. It's easy to get into financial difficulty, often for reasons way beyond your control. Being in debt is not something to be ashamed of. But it is something you need to sort out sooner rather than later. If you are dealing with reputable creditors (e.g. banks, utilities, etc.) then you will discover that they are more flexible than you might imagine and used to dealing with situations far more complex than yours is likely to be. Remember, by acting early you will save yourself a lot of heartache later on. If you feel that you can't cope alone or need to talk to someone, then Credit Action, a registered charity, offer a freephone advice line on 0800 591084.

Second, pay off your debts before you start to save. It's easy to assume that if you've got money in the bank keeping you in the black then you are OK. But the reality is that your debts will need paying eventually and the interest rate on them is almost certainly much higher than that on any savings you have. It's a false economy to be saving while you have significant debt problems; you will only end up chasing an increasingly unreachable target. Commit yourself to paying off as much as you can afford, of any debt, each month. It may be hard work now but it will be worth it in the long run.

Once you're in control of your finances you will be in a far better position to make an informed judgement about how much income you really need each month. This will help you decide whether, and how much, you *need* to work, which, in turn, will help you determine the type of employment you need to secure. There will still be some big questions that you'll need to answer but you'll be well on the way to taking control of your life.

---

**Daphne** (single mum to James, works full time):

However much or little money is available, for me budgeting has been a question of prioritising. A roof over our heads, a fully qualified nanny for James and food in the fridge sit at the top of the list. Recently, money for a nanny has been superseded by the need for school uniform, countless school trips and a never-ending requirement for sports kit.

Working in the wonderful world of media offers me a variety of superficial values – from the car I drive to the shoes I wear. Not succumbing to outside pressures has been a priority and a tough path to follow; I'd rather pay off the mortgage than be seen in the 'right' car or wearing the 'right' shoes.

Having spent a few years recently with less money worries than I had in the early days of being on my own, the pressure will be on to review my spending and work out if part-time or self-employment are options. It's easy to think, 'I'll just get the house decorated' or 'Let's go skiing at Christmas'. – do I really want to prioritise time with James? If I do, I will have to put my money where my mouth is.

Being on your own is really tough when it comes to money; I have no fallback position, and while friends can be really supportive, they can't pay the mortgage or put food in the fridge for me. I think the key is to find someone you can brainstorm with; someone with no axe to grind who can listen and comment positively. This is definitely one I have yet to crack.

---

## Remember

- Never underestimate the financial demands that children bring.
- A budget needn't be complex – it should be an easy way for you to see where your money comes from and goes to.
- If you do the hard work at the beginning, it will require only a small amount of time each month to keep on top of.
- Ignoring financial problems will not make them go away, but being in control of your money will help ease the worries.

## Key principle

**An accurate grasp of your financial position is a key to work/life balance because it helps you appreciate which options are open to you.**

## How to achieve it

- Decide whether to budget on a monthly or weekly basis.
- Work out your net income – see the beginning of this chapter.
- Monitor what you spend over the course of a month.
- Write things down and discover whether you are spending more than you are earning.
- Learn the difference between things you really need and things you can do without.
- Debts are expensive, so work hard to pay them off before trying to save.
- In your calculations, allow for the occasional financial surprise.
- Keep a regular eye on things – a little bit of time each month will make a big difference.

## Basic Budget Template

|  | Amount | Additional info |
|---|---|---|
| **Monthly/weekly income** | | |
| Salary/wages (take home) | | |
| Partner's salary/wages | | |
| Income Support | | |
| Children's Tax Credit | | |
| Working Families' Tax Credit | | |
| Housing Benefit | | |
| Maintenance/Child Support | | |
| Job Seeker's Allowance | | |
| Other | | |
| **TOTAL** | | |

|  | Amount | Additional info |
|---|---|---|
| **Monthly/weekly expenditure** | | |
| Tax (if not taken off already) | | |
| Rent/mortgage | | |
| Council tax | | |
| Water | | |
| Gas | | |
| Electricity | | |
| Phone: landline/mobile | | |

| | Amount | Additional Info |
|---|---|---|
| Food/household needs | | |
| Clothing/shoes | | |
| Maintenance/Child Support | | |
| Children's/school expenses | | |
| Travel expenses | | |
| Car: insurance/tax/petrol/ repairs | | |
| Appliance rental/repairs | | |
| House maintenance | | |
| House insurance | | |
| Leisure activities | | |
| TV licence | | |
| Charitable giving | | |
| Pension | | |
| Life insurance | | |
| Future needs | | |
| Other | | |
| **TOTAL** | | |

**Total income per month/week:**      £ _____

**Total expenditure per month/week:**   £ _____

**Balance for month/week:**      £ _____

# Talk to Your Employer

The chances are that, when you were born, there was no such thing as 'flexible working'. Your mother may well have been given the option of returning to work, indeed she may well have had to, but you can be sure that all the hours would have been agreed to suit the boss with little, if any, thought of the pressures or responsibilities on her. And as for fathers, employers generally made no concessions to family life. If you couldn't do the job in the hours stipulated then the company would simply find someone else who could – the message was a simple one: 'Shape up or ship out!'

It may be a slow process, but the good news is that gradually employers are waking up to the fact that providing flexible working practices for parents not only needn't cost a fortune but that family-friendly working arrangements can actually provide excellent value for money and be good for business. They are learning that, in the long run, happier employees mean happier employers.

**Angela and Stewart** (Angela is at home full time, they have four children, two from Angela's previous relationship)

**Angela**: We had problems when Stewart was working and I was going in and out of hospital. Stewart's boss helped very much and let Stewart take time off as holiday.

When I gave up work after James was born my employer didn't want me to leave. They have always said that there will be a job there for me to come back to. I did try to work part time but it didn't

work for me; I had to travel for three hours to and from work. Although it didn't work for me I know it does work for other people and I am glad that it can.

So if you're about to become a parent for the first time and want, or need, to stay on at work – or if you are already a parent but are struggling to juggle home life with work – now is the time to talk to your employer. You might just be pleasantly surprised by how accommodating they will be. But before you do, follow the three golden rules:

## 1. Check out your options

Before approaching your employer make sure you have thought things through regarding the possible options for, and implications of, changing your established work practices. The trick here is to think about your working options from both sides of the employment fence. Sound out others who've tried different alternatives; decide which is likely to be the best for you and your employer; and then find the right time to make your approach. The most common options are:

- *Full time.* If you don't want the hassle of confronting your boss, continuing on as a full-time member of staff might seem like the easy option for a peaceful life – but that's not necessarily the case. In truth, this option requires as much consideration as any of the alternatives. If you are a single parent, or your partner also works full time, it means that you are going to need childcare arrangements of some description. The problem is that childcare is often less flexible than your employer may be. So if you really want or need to continue to work full time, consider negotiating yourself the same hours but on a flexi-time basis (see below). This may give you the freedom to drop off or pick

up your child from school or childcare while you make alternative arrangements for the other end of the day.
- *Part time.* Reducing your hours down from full time to two or three days a week may seem like an automatic turn-off for your boss. This may be true – not all jobs suit part-time working – but the reality is that, though your employer has no legal obligation to accommodate your request, you may well be viewed as an asset who they would rather have part time than not at all. After all, they have probably invested time and money training you to do your job well, which means that replacing you may involve more hassle than it's worth. The key is to help your employer think through the implications of your reduced hours and where possible to provide answers to their concerns.

If you feel that part-time working is the best option for you then make sure you have covered this in terms of your budget (see Top Tip Four) – you are, after all, going to take a considerable cut in pay. You may also have to face up to the fact that your company may ask you to change your job description to accommodate the reduction in hours. For your employer's benefit, there's a great deal of evidence to suggest that part-time workers have higher productivity, hour on hour, than those working full time.

---

**Daphne** (single mum to James, works full time):

As a single parent I have found this the toughest one of all. Mind games feature highly on my list of barriers to talking to my employer. It's a high-risk game and obviously I can't afford to be out of work. It seems like an uphill task before leaving the starting blocks.

When James was nine years old I knew I had to and wanted to spend more time with him. I'd asked about operating a three-day week but my employer couldn't be flexible. I loved my job but started to look for part-time alternatives, none of which really caught

---

my eye. Eventually, after a quiet weekend away thinking things over, I resigned with no job to go to. (I broke all the sensibility rules and didn't tell my parents first!) My employer knew I didn't want to leave and they didn't want me to leave so we worked out a way for me to change roles and do project work for three days a week. A miracle by any stretch of the imagination!

Eighteen months later, with James installed happily at senior school I needed another challenge. Coincidentally my employer wanted me to set up a department and work full time. That was two years ago and I've gone full circle. Time with James has moved higher up the priority rankings and I need to make a proposal to my employer for the part-time option and be prepared to move on if I can't somehow reduce my hours. The same mind games go on in my head; what compromises can I accept? The stakes are high but I must keep to my priorities.

- *Flexi-time.* One of the biggest misunderstandings about flexi-time is that you get to come and go as you please so long as you eventually make up your hours. The reality is slightly different. Flexi-time is more commonly based around an established 'core' of time stipulated by the employer. Either side of this you can 'flex' your time to suit your needs. So, for example, if you start work late enough to drop your child off at school in the morning you may need to make arrangements to get someone else to pick them up at the end of the day. Though limited, flexi-time does allow you a certain degree of freedom, provided you are able to put forward a viable working arrangement that suits you while ensuring that you can meet your required hours.

    A good selling point to bring to your employers is that, though you get many of the advantages of being part time, they don't have to find anyone to job-share with you, and this will save on their administrative costs. Of course some jobs are more suited to flexi-time than others and so you must think through the specific consequences before you try to persuade your boss that you can make it work for you and them.

- *Job-sharing.* It sounds almost too obvious to say but the biggest obstacle in a job-share is finding the other person who will share your job. This may be easy if you are working in a semi-skilled role, but if you are the chief executive of your company, or a specialist in your field, things may prove a little more difficult. Job-shares can work well but it does take some serious planning and creativity. There are, of course, obvious advantages for your employer. They will not have to find a current employee to cover for you as in the case of part-time working and, unless you can negotiate a flexi-time job-share, the job will still be done during standard working hours or shift patterns for the company. Not only will the business retain your skills, but also your co-worker is likely to bring complementary strengths to the position, making your combined employment even more attractive to your employer.

---

**Catherine and Paul** (married with three children – Paul works full time, Catherine is on a career break)

**Catherine**: As a working parent, I've really benefited from having accommodating and forward-looking employers (the NHS). I think if an organisation is 'officially' sympathetic to parents' needs (I know that not every organisation is), it's more likely that people working in it will also be open to looking more flexibly at the work/home balance.

So far, I've been fortunate to enjoy a range of benefits offered at work – three periods of maternity leave, reduced hours, part-time work, job-sharing, and currently a career break. I've also been able to take carer's leave when necessary and had a short period of using the hospital day nursery when my childcare arrangement broke down.

It is a two-way thing, though, and in return for the flexibility and creativity in accommodating my needs I feel loyal to the NHS and hope I'm regarded as a reliable and conscientious worker.

Even though my employer is 'enlightened', I was still nervous about asking to vary my hours for the first time, so I really prepared myself beforehand. The key thing for me was to show that I knew what I wanted, had thought it through and was prepared to be flexible. This meant doing some homework to show my commitment to making the new arrangement work both for me and for the organisation.

When a colleague in my department and I thought about job-sharing, the first thing we did was to look at the job-sharing policy to make sure we knew what we were letting ourselves in for. Then we spent hours putting together a proposal for the arrangement we'd like. This was also a way of testing out whether or not we felt we could work together well (and happily!). In our document we tried to cover every issue – stressing the good things – two heads better than one, more ideas, more flexibility, etc. – but we also

---

tackled things that can make or break a job-share – how we would share projects, 'seamless' handovers and arrangements for on-call and holiday cover.

By the time we were ready to present our paper, we were confident that it could work, and knowing that helped us to convince our managers that it was a good idea. Everyone was very surprised to see how well prepared we were – we didn't really give them any reason to say no!

It was a lot of talking and paperwork at the time, but it was more than worth all the effort as our managers saw that we were really serious and had thought things through from the organisation's point of view as well as our own.

I think being honest and positive about our reasons for setting up the job-share also helped us. I don't think there is any need to apologise for wanting to balance family and work better and I hope that it gained us more respect as employees. For me that's true for any time you discuss issues related to being a working parent with your employer. If I've had to ask for time off in a crisis, I've often found it so tempting to gloss over the real facts because I feel awkward to admit that it is related (again!) to my children or childcare. In the end, it is much better to be open, admit there's a problem, but that you're ready to do what it takes to sort things out with your employer's support – that way you keep your integrity and reputation as a good employee as well as a caring parent.

- *Compressed hours working.* If you need the benefits of working a three- or four-day week to balance home life with work, but you still need the salary that a full-time position brings in, compressed hours working may provide the solution that you need. Put simply, you work the same number of hours as a normal working week of five days, but you compress them, usually into four days. Be warned, however; this practice is rare and difficult to sell to an employer. As a parent you also have to consider the effect on your home life. Working such long hours may prove to be hard to handle both logistically and emotionally, so weigh this carefully against the positive impact of the time you do spend with your child.

- *Weekend working.* We are fast approaching, and in many cases have already arrived at, the 24/7 week. This opens up the possibility of weekend work, which can be very useful for parents who want to work part time and have a partner who works Monday to Friday, particularly as childcare becomes far less of an issue. However, the pros and cons of this option need to be weighed very carefully as it will inevitably place great constraints on the time you can spend together with your partner and as a family.
- *Term-time working.* There are an increasing number of companies that will employ staff on a full-time basis during school terms only. This flexibility allows parents, especially mothers and single parents, to return to employment in the knowledge that they will not face the difficulties and issues that surround finding supervision for their children during those long school holidays. The main advantage to employers is that they can tap into the vast resource of trained, but otherwise unavailable, parents of school-age children. On the negative side, however, these holidays are usually unpaid.
- *School hours working.* This option is usually offered along with term-time working. It is fantastic if you can find it – not all jobs are suited to hours that fit within the school day, allowing parents to take and pick up their children from school.
- *Home working.* In an age of affordable computing technology, e-mail, Internet, mobile phones and fax machines, the option of working from home, either full time or as a way of making the working day more flexible, has become far more viable. The ability to run your children to school and be available to pick them up again at the end of the day has obvious advantages. However, when your children are very young, looking after them is a

full-time job in itself and so any attempts to work from home before your child goes to school, or during school holidays, are likely to be difficult if not futile. That means you will probably still need to arrange suitable childcare for any children of preschool age.

---

**Andy and Debbie** (Mum and Dad to Sam – Andy works from home, Debbie is a part-time nurse)

**Debbie**: I had planned to have a minimum of six months off from work but after six months I was definitely not ready to return as I was finding motherhood hard and didn't have the confidence or energy to start juggling work and home life. I had already spoken to my manager who was aware that I would not be returning before six months after Sam was born, so she had covered for me by filling my post with someone on a temporary basis. After the six-month period, she was keen for me to keep her informed of when I was planning to return to work so that she had an idea of how to organise her staffing. I probably found it hard to know in advance when I would feel ready to return to work because I was so tired. These symptoms were explained when I was diagnosed with an underactive thyroid gland when Sam was eight months old. Even though I was on maternity leave I felt responsible for my area of work and knew that my indecision would cause problems for my boss, which I in turn found stressful. I eventually returned to work when Sam was ten months old because we felt that financially it was necessary. However, I had also become frustrated by that point with just being a mum and was ready to return to work. My manager was very accommodating and allowed me to return for just two days a week.

**Andy**: During the time that Debbie was thinking of returning to work we didn't want to put Samuel into nursery for more than one day a week. Again because we had no family living nearby, we decided an option would be for me to work a four-day week and to look after Samuel for one day. I approached my manager and was pleased to find out that he was happy to sanction my request. However, shortly after this was agreed I was made redundant. Now that I am self-employed working from home, I am still able to look after Sam every Thursday.

- *Career break*. All the evidence suggests that this is still one of the hardest options to convince an employer to buy into. Employers are reluctant to do this, despite all the statistics that prove it is an extremely cost-effective option for them, particularly if they have already invested time and money in training you to do your job in the first place. If you can manage to persuade your employer to keep your job open then a career break will certainly give you freedom and flexibility. But as with all the other options you have to head into it with your eyes open. The financial cost of a child is huge. Unless you are fortunate enough to have a well-paid partner or significant savings, a career break is probably a non-starter. You also have to accept the fact that unless you can get your employer to agree in writing you would be unlikely to return to a similar position without some form of retraining or refresher course. In this day and age, even taking a couple of years out to raise a family can leave you a long way behind the competition in the employment stakes. You may well be an asset to your company now, but you need to convince them that you will still be in the future.

  Having said all this, you don't have to return to the same company. You might find it more workable to simply take a career break and when you are ready, or need to, offer your skills and experience to other employers.

## 2. Know your rights

Do you know how much maternity leave you are entitled to and when you can start taking it? What about paternity leave? Can you have your job back if you leave to have a child? How will this affect your pay? The legal picture regarding employee rights is complicated and constantly changing. But as a working parent there are certain key issues you should be aware of. For example, did you know that a working mum is entitled to eighteen weeks' maternity leave regardless of whether she is full or part time? This leave can be extended for a further twenty-nine weeks after the baby is born, though there are restrictions on this and your employer can then choose to delay your return if they feel it is inconvenient to them for any reason. As of April 2003, though, ordinary maternity leave may be extended. Check out the government website www.dti.gov.uk/er/index.htm or its interactive site, which helps you to calculate your leave, www.tiger.gov.uk for the latest developments.

Increasingly, employers are coming under pressure to give paternity leave to fathers and some have generous arrangements in place for their staff. At the moment, however, there is no legislation that gives fathers the equivalent of maternity leave although, again, this may be changing in April 2003, so it's all down to how forward-looking your company is. You can, however, claim up to thirteen weeks in the first five years of your child's life under Parental Leave Entitlement, though your employer has no obligation to pay you during this time.

Taking leave from work is just one aspect of the many rights you have as a working parent. You also need to think about your entitlement to Child Benefit, Childcare Tax Credit, Working Families Tax Credit, and so on. For more information on agencies that can help you determine your parental rights, visit www.parentalk.co.uk/atwork.

I'D LOVE TO GUIDE YOUR SLEIGH.. BUT OUR AGREEMENT WAS A WEEK'S NOTICE IN ADVANCE OF OVERTIME.

## 3. Talk to others

Before you stand, knees shaking, lip quivering, ready to tell your boss that you really need to change your working practices for the sake of your sanity and the benefit of your children, check out what you are proposing to say with a friend or two who have already faced the same issues. Thousands of parents, just like you, have been through all the logistics, the soul-searching, the implications and the uncertainties of trying to fit the demands of a job with the priorities of being a parent. So if you think you know what you'd like to do, seek out other parents who have tried it already and get their advice. What sounds great in theory may be a complete nightmare in practice. Unclear expectations, unscrupulous employers, a changing legal picture and the absence of written agreements are just some of the pitfalls that can add to the confusion. By talking to others you will get a much clearer picture of the positives and the negatives of any proposal you are planning to make. The better prepared you are the easier it will be to talk to your employer about how you see things working and the way ahead.

## 4. Making the approach

Your employer needs to be presented with a strong business case for being flexible in their working practices. The major factor that is likely to swing your case will be if you are already valued as a conscientious worker. Large organisations may already have helpful policies in place and the facilities and staffing levels to make them work. Smaller businesses may need more convincing and will be justifiably concerned that adopting your preferred option may well benefit you, but only at the expense of the company. So:

- *Do your homework.* The best way to make a business case for flexible working is to arm yourself with as much information as possible about how the particular scheme you are proposing operates. Do your homework on how it will affect your particular situation as an employee as well as the implications for your employer. Remember, there isn't a one-size-fits-all option. Each employer/employee relationship is unique, so make sure you've thought through the appropriate issues before you make your approach.
- *Write your proposal down.* Writing down your proposal is a good thing to do for several reasons. First, it will clarify your thinking for your own purposes. Second, when you finally get to speak to your boss it will help you to be clear and precise in what you are suggesting. And finally, you will also have a hard copy of your proposal to present to them, which they can then refer to later for clarification of what you are suggesting.
- *Find a good time for your boss.* It's no good sidling up to your boss by the coffee machine just as they are about to go into an important meeting. A casual corridor chat will not give the impression that you are serious about your proposals. Be as official as is possible within your company's culture. Make an appointment that will give you long enough to put your case, listen to any reservations your boss may have and talk things through.
- *Present your case.* Just as you had to sell yourself to get your job in the first place, you will now have to sell yourself again. Play to your strengths. Remind your boss

about your proven ability to do the work. At the end of the day, even if your employer is unconvinced about some kind of flexible working pattern, they know that it may come down to going with it as the 'lesser of two evils'. As an employer myself I know that it is far better to work flexibly with proven staff than to try to find a new employee who may need considerable training as well as time to settle into the job and adapt to the specific way the organisation runs.

- *Be positive about why you want to do this.* Flexible working is about benefits not favours. You are not asking your boss for a favour – so always sell your idea in a language that speaks about 'benefits' – especially the benefits to your employer. That way you stand a much better chance of being taken seriously. And remember, you don't have to apologise for being a parent.
- *Pre-empt their questions.* If you've done your homework, thought things through, and written down your proposal then there is no reason why you should get caught out as you speak to your boss. Being prepared will help you to pre-empt their questions and reservations as well as to answer those that are asked positively, clearly and confidently. This will not only help to put your employer at ease but also give you the best chance of coming away with the desired result.

It should be clear from this chapter that if you need, or want, to return to work after the birth of your child then there are plenty of options available for you to do so. But in all of them one of the key issues for consideration in making your decision is how to make sure your child is well cared for while you are at work. Because suitable childcare is essential when it comes to planning your career options, just before you go rushing off to speak to your boss, take a look at the next chapter.

**John** (Dad to Pearse, works from home while his wife works abroad):

I was about to say that since I'm freelance this bit doesn't apply to me. Then I remembered that the very fact that freelancers don't have set working hours means that left to our own devices, we're highly likely to work far more hours than we would if we had an employer . . . that's certainly a pattern I've fallen into in the past. As always I have tended to use my family as an excuse – 'I may not get any other work this year, so I'd better grab it all now to make sure I can cover the school fees' – when actually my family are the ones who suffer when I overwork. If I did have an employer at least I could blame them for making me overwork . . . Because I'm self-employed, my son, who is by his nature very logical, can conclude only that since how I spend my hours is my decision, it follows that if I choose to spend them all working, work must be a lot more interesting to me than he is.

One day I looked in the mirror and had a long talk with my employer. Luckily he was very supportive of my wanting to spend more time on things that really mattered. But, hey, he's a family man himself.

## Remember

- Employers are beginning to recognise the mutual benefits of flexible working.
- You are an asset to your employer, and one in which they will have already invested significant time and money.
- There is a host of different ways to vary your working pattern, but not all will be suitable for all jobs.
- A good existing relationship with your boss, and a reputation as a conscientious employee is the best starting point for talking about flexible working arrangements.
- In raising the issue of flexible working, you are not asking a favour. Instead you are pointing out the benefits of a change in work patterns to you and the business.
- There is a lot of evidence to suggest that employers get better productivity from part-time employees than from full-time ones.

## Key principle

**Talk to your employer about the options open to you as a working parent – you may find them to be more flexible than you imagine.**

## How to achieve it

- Check out the options before approaching your employer.
- Know your rights as an employee.
- Talk to family and friends before talking to your boss.
- Talk to other acquaintances who have tried the flexible working option that you want.
- Think about your employer's point of view as well as your own.
- Always emphasise the positive benefits to your employer.
- Write your proposal down.
- Find the right time to talk to your employer, so that neither they nor you feel rushed.

**Top Tip Six**

# Choose Childcare that You're Really Happy With

You need only one goal when choosing childcare – and that's to *choose childcare that you're really happy with*. If you are planning to return to work you need to take seriously the responsibility of making sure you get the sort of childcare that will mean your child is safe and stimulated, which will give you peace of mind. The problem is that when you are pushed for time, confused by the options, overwhelmed by the red tape and counting the cost, it's all too easy to feel rushed into settling for second-best. It's a huge mistake to presume that every childcare facility or agency is as good as the next. They vary, not only in the type of care they offer but also in quality, facilities, cost and style.

Getting childcare you're really happy with means putting in some serious legwork as soon as possible. Delay will only increase the risk of frustrating waiting lists or the disappointment and uncertainty of having to cope with second-best – which you will then constantly worry about until you can eventually put it right, adding yet more pressure to an already hectic life. And though you will inevitably worry about leaving your child with childcarers, all the research shows that there are many positive benefits of childcare, including the ability of children to relate better to other children, confidence-building and an easier transition into school life. This should help you to be a little easier on yourself when the inevitable feelings of guilt at having to leave your child set in.

So what are your options? What are the pros and cons of each form of childcare? How can you be sure that you are asking the right questions? And where can you look for help?

## Check out the options

Below is an overview of childcare options, mostly suitable for younger children. Not all of these will necessarily be available in your area, however, so for more information about childcare options in your locality contact Childcare Link on 08000 96 02 96 or visit their website at www.childcarelink.gov.uk.

### 1. Day nurseries

Day nurseries cater for children aged from six weeks to five years. There are various types of day nursery, which can be privately, community-, council- or workplace-run. All must be regularly inspected and comply with the Office for Standards in Education (OFSTED) regulations, which include strict guidelines on staff/children ratios:

- Under twos – one carer to three children
- Two- to three-year-olds – one carer to four children
- Three- to five-year-olds – one carer to eight children.

Because these nurseries are specifically aimed at providing a service for working parents, the hours they open will generally coincide with the average working day – 8 a.m. to 6 p.m. They also open all year round. If you can find a good local authority nursery you may find that it is free. However, there is normally a cost – and it is rarely cheap, especially if you need your child cared for all week.

Day nurseries are a good choice if:

- you would prefer your child to be looked after by professionals;
- you want 100 per cent reliability from your childcare;
- you want continuity of care over several years.

They are not so good if:

- you work flexible hours;
- your nursery is not near work or home and you need to combine it with the school run for your older children;
- you have no back-up plans for emergencies – you can't take your child to nursery if they are ill.

---

**Andy and Debbie** (Mum and Dad to Sam – Andy works from home, Debbie is a part-time nurse):

We were fussy about childcare and preferably we would have liked our family to look after our son but unfortunately they lived too far away. We looked at childminding as this was the cheaper option but we had no one personally recommended and we were concerned about what would happen if the childminder became ill or was on holiday and wasn't able to look after our son. The absence of nearby family to help in these situations caused us to look for other solutions. We were not happy for Samuel to go to somebody we didn't know well.

When we looked at nurseries we were initially particularly fussy about cleanliness and friendliness but were also keen for Samuel to be with other children of the same age.

---

## 2. Childminders

Paid on an hourly basis, childminders are self-employed and use their own homes. The cost, hours, terms and conditions are usually negotiated directly with each parent. As with day nurseries, childminders must be registered with OFSTED who will make annual visits to the minder and their home to ensure suitability. They are also subject to police checks, as are any other adults who may be around in their home during the day. A childminder is limited in the number of children they can supervise – six children under eight (under twelve in Scotland

and Northern Ireland), of which only three can be under five, and only one under the age of one, although special exceptions can sometimes be made for siblings. This includes the child-minders' own children.

Childminders are a good choice if:

- you work irregular hours;
- you have children of different ages and you would like them to be together;
- you would like a home environment for your child.

They are not so good if:

- you think your child may need more space or more stimulation with other children.

The National Childminding Association can provide you with more help and advice. Contact them on 0800 169 4486.

---

**John** (Dad to Pearse, works from home while his wife works abroad):

My wife has a large family of live-in brothers and sisters, and I must admit that coming from a small family myself, I found all the comings and goings, queues for the bathroom and engaged telephone lines a bit much to cope with. But that all changed as soon as our son was born. I realised that these people weren't teenagers; they were baby-sitters! So even though my wife spends a lot of time overseas, and I'm the main carer, I would never compare my lot with a regular single parent.

At my son's school I have met a couple of people who have to combine work with parenting with almost no support and I really do take my hat off to them. In my case, there's hardly ever a time when there isn't another responsible person on hand to take charge of my son when I need to work or occasionally socialise. I say

---

'occasionally' because as my son gets older we have a more 'pally' relationship and there are many times that my favourite social activity is the two of us spending time together . . . only trouble is he always wants to go to his cousins' houses where they have better pizzas and DVDs!

Seriously, I'm very happy that he feels comfortable staying in a number of homes. I think it will stand him in good stead in later life – I recall I spent most of my childhood glued to my mum! It's worth pointing out though, that coming from a smaller family it took me a while to get comfortable asking for childcare help . . . I thought there was great virtue in slogging on by myself. Now that I've got over that hurdle I am very happy to tap into the childcaring resources my extended family provides . . . and of course I try to remember to take my turn at having the rest of Pearse's cousins over to give other families a break too.

## 3. Nannies

In some ways a nanny is much the same as a childminder except that you employ them directly to look after your child in your own home. There is no legal requirement for you to employ a nanny with any formal qualifications in childcare and they aren't inspected by OFSTED, unless they're looking after two or more families. You may want to choose a nanny with a nursery nursing diploma (NNEB) but the responsibility to choose a suitable nanny for your child is entirely yours. It's up to you to do the interviewing and checking. For some people, especially those who work full time, a live-in nanny is a good option, but the most common arrangement is the live-out variety who work a set number of days and hours. One way of cutting costs and employing someone suitable might be to share a nanny with another family.

Nannies are a good choice if:

- you want a high level of input into how your child is looked after;

- you would like someone to fit in around the hours that you work;
- you believe your child would feel more secure within your home environment;
- you have more than one child.

They are not so good if:

- you think your child would prefer to be around other children;
- you don't want the burden of sorting out contracts regarding hours, sick pay, holidays, etc.;
- you would like your childcare to be consistent – good nannies will eventually move on – sometimes sooner, rather than later;
- you are eligible for payment of some childcare costs through Childcare Tax Credit – it doesn't cover unregistered childcare like nannies who work for only one family. (For information about eligibility for Childcare Tax Credit see below under 'Check out the cost'.

---

**Daphne** (single mum to James, works full time):

Once I knew that I'd be working full time the job of sorting out childcare became a priority. For anyone who has suffered from a bad back and received vast amounts of well-intentioned advice about 'what you need' I can assure you there is as much advice about childcare. Each set of circumstances is unique. I had to decide – with my husband who was still around at the time – what suited us the best. I read a superb book that set out all the alternatives, together with likely costs. The thing I took to heart the most was one comment: you don't employ your accountant to clean your house and vice versa. I was sure that I wanted a nanny who was qualified and dedicated to our – as yet unborn – child.

---

Our advertisement, carefully drawn up to a clear brief, gave rise to one – yes, one – response! We promised not to take her on just because she was the sole applicant. We interviewed Justine and she seemed great for the job; she answered all our prepared questions and had sensible questions of her own. I'm not sure that recruitment consultants would recommend it as part of the decision-making process but when our normally shy cat jumped onto her lap that sealed the deal! Justine stayed with us for better and worse for four years.

Following Justine's departure, and after a pretty disastrous six months of a nanny-share, I realised that for my situation a live-in nanny was the best option. I had a much better response this time, through a couple of agencies. I decided that interviews would include an overnight stop. What a great decision that was! After a surprising start – me having been interviewed by a pretty forthright parent at Euston Station! – our third applicant was a complete hit. In the morning I couldn't find James as he was ensconced with Rachel. She stayed with us for eight years, including a house move, and still lives near us as part of our extended family.

One thing that's worked particularly well has been flexibility for both my nannies. After a period of settling, they both cared for other children as well as James, in order to keep up their level of interest (and revenue). We worked out a way for Justine to go to college before moving on to teacher training college when she left us. Rachel worked at James' junior school as the nursery nurse and has been able to stay there since leaving us.

## 4. Nursery schools

It's easy to confuse nursery schools with day nurseries (discussed above). However, unlike day nurseries, which open for the duration of the working day, nursery school hours are typically 9 a.m. to 3.30 p.m. and during term-time only. There is, however, some flexibility in that your child may be able to attend for just the morning or afternoon. All are registered and inspected by OFSTED. Again, cost can vary. If privately run, there will be a financial burden to cover. There are, however, many nursery schools run as part of the state education system, which are free. Check out the age range that any nursery covers, as this will vary, with some taking children as young as six months and others only taking toddlers through to school age.

Nursery schools are a good choice if:

- you are looking for good childcare at a reasonable cost;
- you would like your child to get the opportunity to mix with other similar-aged children;
- you work within nursery hours.

They are not so good if:

- your working hours won't fit in around the nursery hours;
- you feel that your child may not be quite ready for the structure of a school nursery.

## 5. Playgroups and preschools

For children aged between three and five, playgroups and preschools offer educational and play facilities. They tend to operate out of community centres, church halls or similar communal buildings, which means that finding one close to your home shouldn't be a problem, though you may need to put your child's name down some time in advance. They must be run by trained playgroup leaders and parents and are OFSTED-inspected to ensure professional standards. The typical day is broken down into sessions of two to three hours, giving you the flexibility of being able to leave your child there for part or all of the day. Cost is usually per session, though most playgroups and preschools have a policy of asking for a block booking, paid in advance, in order to control numbers of attendees.

Playgroups and preschools are a good choice if:

- you would like your child to mix with others;
- you would like your child to have access to a variety of toys, equipment and other stimulation;
- you would like to meet other parents who take their children and may stay with them throughout the session;
- you would like to get involved with the playgroup yourself.

They are not so good if:

- you need more flexibility.

## 6. After-school 'latchkey' care

Sometimes known as Kids' Clubs, after-school 'latchkey' care offers safe after-school and holiday supervision for children from primary age right through to the first few years of secondary education. They are usually based in community or youth centres or may be held on school premises. If your child's school isn't home to an after-school club, don't panic. Childcare workers often collect children from different schools and take them directly to the club. For added safety all children are registered on arrival and not signed out until the parent or a known and designated representative collects them. Pick-up time for after-school care is usually 6 p.m. Cost can vary dramatically depending on the provider, so shop around. All after-school clubs and holiday clubs are inspected by OFSTED.

For parents who need to be at work early there has also been a recent trend towards offering breakfast club facilities, usually starting around 8.00 a.m.

After-school 'latchkey' care is a good choice if:

- you aren't able to collect your child from school;
- you've got older children and you would like them to be supervised by adults.

It's not so good if:

- you need flexibility;
- your child gets so tired after school that all they want to do is to go home;
- your child is uncertain about mixing with other age groups.

## Check out the cost

Almost all childcare involves some kind of cost, but the financial outlay can vary quite considerably. Make sure you've budgeted carefully and know what you can (and more importantly, *can't*) afford. If you don't know, go back to Top Tip Four and find out. To find out about benefits, including free places for three- and four-year-olds, contact: The Children's Tax Credit Helpline: 0845 300 1036; or Working Families Tax Credit Hotline: 0845 609 5000.

## Ask lots of questions

With the exception of your own personal nanny, the Office for Standards in Education (OFSTED) are responsible for checking, registering, inspecting and reviewing all other childcare facilities and personnel. That means that your potential childcare provider has to meet a set of national standards, including those of health and safety, care and learning provision. However, don't just leave it to the inspectors. The best safety net your child has is your ongoing concern for their well-being while they are out of your direct care. So, before you sign on the dotted line, make sure that you ask plenty of searching questions. Here are a few to get you thinking:

## Questions for providers

### *1. Day nurseries/nurseries/nursery schools/playgroups and preschools*

- What will your child's day involve?
- What is the ratio of carers to children?
- Do they operate a 'key carer' system, where one person will have main responsibility for your child and for building a relationship with them?
- Is there any opportunity to talk with the carer at the beginning and/or end of the day?
- How many staff are qualified or experienced?
- How open are the staff to your being present, getting involved occasionally and asking questions?

### *2. Childminders*

- How long have they been doing the job?
- Will they be happy to provide references from other parents for whom they have worked?
- Do they have other children to care for? If so, what ages?
- Would they seek to provide any structure to your child's time with them?
- Are they registered with OFSTED?
- Would they be happy to provide a short daily or weekly report about their activities with your child?

### 3. Nannies
- What experience and/or qualifications do they have?
- Are they happy with the job profile (that you should have drawn up as a basis for your relationship)? Are there some things on it that they particularly like or dislike?
- Will they be happy to provide references?
- Why do they want this job?
- Will they be prepared to report back each day or week on the structure of each day?

## Questions for other parents who use the same childcare
- What has been their experience?
- Any problems?
- Any really positive comments?
- Ask them about any concerns that you may have.

## Questions for yourself
As well as asking questions of those who will be looking after your child, and talking to other people who currently use the same childcare that you are considering using, it's important to ask *yourself* some questions too. It's easy to assume that, once you've found the place for your child, from there on in, you'll be able to enjoy a stress-free life as a working parent. Of course the truth is that, as with any relationship, the one with your carer will require hard work and constant communication if it is to work well for everyone involved. The last thing you'll need is for your childcare arrangements to be an added source of pressure, so ask yourself:

- Am I willing to be honest with the carer from day one and talk about any concerns I have as they arise?
- Am I being realistic about the time pressures facing me, so that I don't find myself just dumping my child and not giving them the time they need to settle into the day?
- Do I have a clear and accurate idea of the hours that I

need childcare arranged for? You need to take into account the travelling time between the place where your child is being cared for and your own place of work. Be realistic. Being consistently unable to get there when you say you will only adds more stress to your, your carer's and your child's day.

• Am I taking a genuine and regular interest in my child's care? Regularly talk to the carer about how your child is getting on and listen to what they have to say.

---

**Angela and Stewart** (Angela is at home full time, they have four children, two from Angela's previous relationship)

**Angela**: Childcare has been a very important issue for us. We found no childcare for children with special needs, which is why I haven't gone back to work after having Denise, and as we had to cope with hospital appointments with her not being very well we decided it was best for me to stay at home.

---

## Be prepared to change if it doesn't work out

Clearly, unnecessarily changing your childcare arrangements is something you will want to avoid. Too many changes are bound to have a negative effect on your child. However, if you are unhappy with aspects of the care your child is receiving you must take action straightaway. Never sweep real issues under the carpet. Here's what to do:

- Raise the issue as soon as you can with the carer. Explain clearly why you are concerned, but also suggest some positive ways in which the situation can be sorted out.
- Listen to what the carer says, but if you're not happy, stick to your guns until you are.
- Agree an action plan with the carer.
- Always remain calm, and try to set out the issues as carefully and objectively as you can. That said, you know your child better than anyone – and they are your responsibility – so don't give up on the issue until it is truly resolved.
- If you're still not happy, check out your rights. Make sure that you're familiar with any notice period that you have agreed and give some thought to any temporary childcare that you may need to arrange until you can find something more permanent.

---

**Catherine and Paul** (married with three children – Paul works full time, Catherine is on a career break)

**Catherine**: Finding the right childcare has been the single most crucial thing for us as working parents. If you're not happy with your childcare and spend your time fretting about your children, you just can't perform well, never mind enjoy your job!

We found getting the right care at the right price in the right place for the right hours is a huge challenge that requires a lot of effort!

---

Now with three children, we look back to when we were organising care for our first baby and think how straightforward that sounds. We wanted to have a live-out nanny so our son could be in his own home, so the first step was to join an agency and put an advert in the professional nanny magazines. We were surprised at how much all this cost, but in the end it paid off and, via our advert, we found a newly qualified nanny with loads of energy and enthusiasm.

Some of my friends obviously disapproved of me leaving my precious baby in the care of a nineteen-year-old, but I liked and trusted her from the beginning and the arrangement was a great success. Luke was cared for beautifully and had lots of fun and friends. We were sad, although not surprised, when she left to train as a teacher.

Once he was two, Luke started at a nursery, which was probably the least stressful childcare situation we've had. I loved the feel of the nursery from the moment I visited; everything seemed well run, secure and consistent. I liked and respected the owner and the staff who were professional and affectionate towards the children. All our children have since been to the same nursery and had a great time.

Good nurseries do get very booked up so my advice is to visit and put your child's name down early if you like somewhere – you can always take it off if you change your mind.

After baby number two, and with me working part time, we went back to having a nanny who we found through an agency. Again, we were fortunate to find someone who we liked and who helped us through a number of life's events in the following two years.

We found that gut feelings were very important when recruiting a nanny as well as asking all the practical questions. You have to like and trust someone completely if it's going to work so following up references is vital. We've always had proper contracts with our nannies as well as paying their tax and national insurance contributions, which does add up financially and means a lot of paperwork. But doing it properly is worth it if that's the arrangement you want for your children.

After such a good run, it was a 'crisis' of childcare that spurred me on to take a career break. We'd had our third baby, Titus, and our nanny returned for two days a week, but her circumstances had changed as well as ours – she was a mum now and had moved further away. It was soon obvious that the arrangement was very stressful all round so we mutually agreed that she would leave.

Looking for childcare for three children was not easy, especially at short notice, but we set up a temporary arrangement with a lovely childminder who I already knew, to allow me to work my notice.

Now that I'm thinking of returning to work sometime next year, I will approach the whole issue differently, probably fitting any work around my childcare – which could mean some big changes and no doubt, many more challenges!

## Never view childcare as a replacement for your time

Finding good childcare doesn't let you off the hook when it comes to spending quality time with your child. Don't fall into the trap of thinking that they have had enough stories, games, conversation or stimulation for the day. They need you: *your* time; *your* interest; *your* love. And they need it now! In the light of all the other demands on your time and energy, reading to your child each night or taking them to play on the swings in the park at the weekend may not seem like a particularly high priority, but it is exactly what they desperately need. Never forget, all children spell love T-I-M-E. Your child needs you to make a clear distinction between your work and being their mother or father. So for all those important top tips on finding that vital time for your child, read on.

## Remember

- There are many positive benefits of childcare.
- Resist the temptation to go for childcare that you really cannot afford.
- Even the best childcare can have occasional hiccups with illnesses, etc., so – before trouble hits – think about a 'plan B' that you can employ if necessary.
- Trust your judgement – remember that you know your child best.
- Be honest with yourself and the carer about the daily time pressures that you face.
- Don't be afraid to keep asking lots of questions until you're completely happy.
- Childcare – however good – can never (and should never) replace you, so continue to make time with your child a priority.

## Key principle

**Childcare that you're uncertain about only adds to a stressful day for you and your child, so do your home-work, ask lots of questions, be honest from day one and trust your judgement.**

## How to achieve it

- Try to avoid rushing into choosing childcare.
- Start looking sooner rather than later.
- Check out the options and make a list.
- If appropriate, go and visit and ask lots of questions.
- Check out the fine print.
- Make your choice.
- Make sure you get something in writing.
- Always be honest with the carer about any issues as they arise.
- Don't be afraid to change your childcare if you're unhappy.

**Part Three**

# Making It Work

# Make a Clear Division between Work and You

In our global, broadband, digital, contact-driven, 24/7 society it's harder than ever to avoid the temptation, indeed the overwhelming pressure, to extend the working day just that little bit longer or to take your day's work home with you. Phone calls need to be made, e-mails checked and reports written – now! It's all too easy to take on the extra shift, answer just one more call or finish off typing up those letters at home over the weekend. The global marketplace does not respect time zones or parents' needs for quality, relaxed time with their family. But as working practices change faster than ever before, with many of us carrying our entire office in our briefcases, it is even more important for both you and your child that you make a clear division between work and home. So just how do you do it?

## Get in the real world

The truth is it can be impossible to separate work from home. Even if we don't literally bring work home in our briefcase, many of us bring it home in our heads, which can be just as distracting when it comes to really 'being there' for our family.

For most of us, the boundaries between our home and work life are bound to get blurred. So rather than trying to achieve the impossible – and end up defeated and depressed – what you really need to avoid is the total blurring of your work and *you*. You don't need to be defined by what you do. Your child needs you, the parent, not a 'full-time' secretary, account-ant, engineer, administrator, building contractor, shop assistant or bus driver who just happens to share a home with them. We've all got friends who have let their work become their life. They never switch off, they rarely talk about anything else other than business and they bring their work home with them, even when it's not necessary – in short the single issue of what they do for a living shapes their whole identity. They end up not so much human *beings* as human *doings*!

I WISH YOU'D STOP BRINGING YOUR WORK HOME WITH YOU.

Of course, we live in the real world and that means that many of us, on a regular basis, have to work overtime or at weekends, bring work home with us or at the very least be available on the end of a mobile phone. You'll never succeed as a working parent if you spend your life beating yourself up about responsibilities that you can't shed. I would love to be able to work part time, or at the very least fit my job into a comfortable nine-to-five, with every weekend off and six weeks' holiday a year. The reality, however, is that I am responsible for a large international charity, which employs hundreds of staff. My commitment to making that organisation work and safeguarding (as best I can) the living of my staff inevitably means that work spills over virtually every day into my home life. But precisely because of that fact, I also have to remember that I have a commitment to my wife and my family to be as hard-working a husband and father as I am an employer.

Every child needs parents who live life in a way that lets them know they are loved, and that they are their number-one priority. And the only way to achieve this is through giving them time – in quantity and quality. And that means a commitment to working hard to get the balance right between work and you, and making it a priority now.

---

**Debbie and Andy** (Mum and Dad to Sam – Andy works from home, Debbie is a part-time nurse)

**Andy**: It was probably easier for Debbie to split time at work with time with Sam as she had two specific shifts that she was required to work. The majority of the time she isn't required to bring work home with her.

I found it more difficult initially as my job required me to travel to London from our home in Leicester two or three days a week. Because I also worked from home and there was always work to be done I found it much harder to be available to Samuel and Debbie during particularly stressful times.

After about six months I realised that I had been putting work ahead of my family. I decided to try to work more flexibly so that I could be available at the times of the day when Samuel and Debbie really needed me. After about nine months I changed my job and became self-employed. This gave me much more flexibility and I decided to work a four-day week. This enabled me to look after Sam on one of the two days that Debbie had to work. Sam went to a nursery on the other day.

Over the months I have had to adapt to a different way of working to support Debbie through some difficult days. I used to prefer to work uninterrupted but have learnt to cope with being more flexible.

---

## Work constructively

David is a 39-year-old maths teacher and the father of two children. Like all teachers, David works long hours, often working into the evening and at weekends marking books and planning lessons. And despite the fact that his holidays always coincide with his children's, he still has to be careful about workloads that can so often eat away at that all-too-precious family time. Added to that, David has recently taken on the role of departmental head, which has meant extra duties. Despite talking through the implications with his family before accepting this promotion, things haven't been easy.

'It's rather ironic being a teacher and a parent as you spend far more hours with other people's children than you do with your own,' David reflects. 'And of course, once the children have left for the day to go home, there is still all the paperwork that has to be done and the preparations to be made for the following day's lessons or even the next term. I try not to stay too late at school but the reality is, if you don't put the hours in, then it seriously affects your ability to do the job, no matter how many years you have been teaching.'

David's secret to succeeding as a working parent though, is not to let the demands of work take over completely, but instead to adapt the strategies that have made him a good teacher and apply them to his home life.

'Cutting corners is never an option at work, but experience tells you what needs to be done and what can wait. I can also see that children respond positively when you have time for them. This has really inspired and encouraged me in my home life. I've learnt the lesson that if I can prioritise things when it comes to work then I can do the same when it comes to my family. I often have work that cannot wait, which means working at weekends and during holidays. But always I try to plan and organise my work cleverly so that it doesn't interfere with my life as a parent to two active children.'

Making a clear division between work and you is all about prioritising and being willing to make the tough decisions that balance the demands of work and home. If you've got work hanging over you at the beginning of a holiday, don't try to sweep it under the carpet. If it simply can't wait then, as the immortal slogan of a leading sports company suggests, *Just do it!* After all, I'm sure that as a parent you'd give the same advice to your children if they had homework that needed doing during the holidays. Don't beat yourself up about something you can do nothing about or stick your head in the sand and pretend it's not there. It will only come back to haunt you. Instead, plan, organise and schedule so you can get the work done in an efficient but unobtrusive way. If you have a young child, then an hour in the evening when they have gone to bed or even during their afternoon sleep may be an ideal time. If your child is older, particularly in their teenage years, then the chances are they won't rise much before mid-morning! This gives you the chance to have a leisurely breakfast and do an hour or two's work without depriving them of any of your attention at all.

In our organisation we used to have a rule that when you were on holiday you were not allowed to phone in to the office. That way, the theory went, you would have to let things rest until your return and so have a good, relaxing and enjoyable break. The rule was nonsense! I can't tell you how many holidays I spent worrying about the fact that on the last day in the office I forgot to pass on an important piece of information, which meant that not only was work more stressful on my return for myself and my colleagues, but I carried that fact with me the whole time I was away. A simple phone call would have made life easier for my colleagues, my family and me. We've now dropped the 'Don't contact the office' rule. This means, of course, that for the first couple of days or so of my holiday I remember things from time to time that I need to ring the office about. But it also means that I'm far more relaxed and more fun to be with.

However, while dealing with work that needs to be done

has its benefits, never let work interfere where it doesn't have to. If something *can* wait then let it wait. It may mean you have a slightly heavier workload when you return after the weekend or a holiday, but that's far preferable to having a family who think they always come second to the company or your clients – and have plenty of evidence to prove it.

Just as you can't always take phone calls while you are at work because you are busy giving your attention to the job at hand or because you are in a meeting, don't forget that it's OK to operate the same principle at home. Take deliberate steps to ensure you have uninterrupted time with your family whenever possible. Turn the phone off, forget the e-mails and ignore the fax machine! And if you're going out, leave the mobile phone on the kitchen table so it won't be a temptation to you.

The truth is, while technology has made life easier for us it has also had the strange effect of turning our priorities upside down. Why, for example, will we always pick up the phone and allow it to interrupt whatever we are doing despite the fact that the caller, more often than not, only wishes to discuss something that could wait or turns out to be frustratingly trivial?

Yet a letter, which generally has had more thought put into it and is therefore more likely to be of some importance, we leave to one side to be buried under a pile of other paper! We just don't prioritise in a way that makes sense.

Most of us will spend forty years working before we retire. That's a long time in which to make an impact in the world of employment. Yet the formative years of your child's life, the most fruitful opportunity you have to spend time with them and influence them, is gone in under half that time. The childhood years are fleeting, so seize the day, because your children will soon be grown and gone, embarking on their own careers and priorities. If they aren't a big part of your life now, don't expect to be a huge part of their lives then.

---

**Catherine and Paul** (married with three children – Paul works full time, Catherine is on a career break)

**Paul**: I've always been involved with the children in a 'hands-on' way – as far as my time would allow. I love being with them and in previous jobs, when Catherine was working, I'd happily step in with childcare. Things have changed a bit now, though, as I now have a more senior role and not so much flexibility. In theory, I'm on call all the time.

When I agreed to take the new job, we talked about the implications for our family life. Catherine had decided to be at home for a while, so we knew there would be more continuity for the children, but making the adjustment hasn't been easy. The main drawback is the unpredictability of being on call and knowing that plans often have to be changed at short notice if I'm needed to sort out a problem at work.

We've always made an effort to keep time off 'sacred' and weekends tend to revolve around family activities. Our house is still far from finished and our home 'in-tray' spills into several rooms. We like to think we're still perfectionists 'in theory' but family time must be our priority at the moment.

---

I've sometimes had to cancel or change days off, which disappoints all of us and causes general inconvenience. We're learning now, though, not to think of it as the end of the world, but just to get on and reschedule as soon as possible. If my mobile goes off on a Saturday morning there is usually a silent 'sigh' and a sinking feeling – we all now know what it could mean for our weekend.

Finding time to do things individually with our three children is a challenge, but we do our best. Luke, our nine-year-old, is into sports and activities so my special times with him are spent swimming, playing tennis, cricket, etc. – and just 'being' together. This is really precious to me and I feel that it's a wonderful investment for our relationship as he grows up.

When I travel abroad, I miss my family terribly. I know that the children are unsettled until I'm home again so I try to call home when they're still up and around for a chat – it's good catching up with their days and telling them about mine. I don't buy expensive gifts but always try to bring something home just to let them know that I've been thinking about them – and not just work – while I've been away. If possible, I plan a day off soon after a trip away.

The new job has put added strain on us as a couple. When I'm working late or away, Catherine has to hold things together – I don't underestimate that, especially when she's been looking after the children all day. I sometimes bring work home, which also eats into our time together. We moan about it, but accept it and try to find at least some 'us' time before we go to bed. We find too that planning and enjoying an evening out together as often as we can helps to compensate for hours working late, away or in front of the computer at home.

I talk about my work at home and our children know all the 'characters'. Visiting the office in the holidays is a special treat. I'm proud of them and they've never let me down yet (although I say only nice things about colleagues in front of them!). I think it's good for people at work to see me as a 'whole' person and in action as a dad. It helps, at least, to explain the occasional puffy eyelids, snotty suit sleeve, Weetabix shirt and grey hairs!

## Communicate clearly

At the end of the day, making a clear division between work and you is, first, about making clear *decisions*, in your own mind, about how work fits in around your family; and, second, about clear *communication* to your family about precisely where work starts and stops, emphasising how important they are to you.

It's sometimes hard to believe but you really are a huge influence on your children. It may not seem like it when they don't dress the way you'd want them to, their taste in music leaves a lot to be desired and they constantly use phrases such as, 'You're so old-fashioned', 'George's mum always lets him go to the cinema on his own' or 'Rosie's dad never makes her tidy up her room.' But the truth is, they need you. If you were to suddenly disappear their world would come crashing down around them. You are the most important role model your children will ever have. Though at times their behaviour may suggest something very different, they love you and desperately need you to love them and to make it plain. So take time to consider what you are modelling and communicating to them.

You may think that working all hours to provide your kids with everything you never had as a child is a clear demonstration of your love, and that they understand the concept, 'I'm doing this for you.' But in reality, if all you do is work, work, work, however much you give to your child in terms of material things they will still believe that what's most important to you is your job and not them. Their understanding of the world is simple and accurate; if you love someone then you automatically want to spend time with them. And the sad fact is, if you are never there for them because you are always at work, history may repeat itself. Your own children may well grow up to believe that being a parent is all about providing and so end up just as absent from their child as you are from them.

As a parent you need to demonstrate to your kids that success as a working parent is not about how high you can climb the career ladder but about achieving a healthy balance between the necessities of earning a living and the priorities of investing time in those you love.

---

**John** (Dad to Pearse, works from home while his wife works abroad):

Some time ago I became a Christian and, since then, it's been a lot easier to make a division between work and home, on a Sunday anyway. But I have realised that there needs to be a division between work and church time too – after all, whether I'm busy with a contract or preparing a service, to a seven-year-old it all still looks like I have no time for him. As a freelancer I've always got pressing deadlines – some of which extend way after coming-home-from-school time, so I've found the best way to cope is a combination of explanation and planning. My son already knows what a print deadline is, so that even though I may have to send a fax or an e-mail before working on his homework with him, it's not that the fax is more important, it's just that it's more time-sensitive. If, as usually happens, there's a glitch during the school run, I think he quite enjoys the mad dashing round the high street to try to find a fax machine to re-send the missing article or e-mail.

When we get home we make a plan – 'You get your school clothes off, have a snack and watch some TV and I'll get another hour of work done – then we'll play in the park and make a start on your homework.' As long as my son is confident that I'll keep to my part of the agreement he'll usually keep to his and I can work undisturbed. Sometimes the work I have to do won't fit into the hour available, but I've found it's much better to break, spend time with him when I've promised to and return to work later. Besides keeping my word, and letting Pearse know my work isn't more important than him, the mental break is often really helpful in returning to the computer with fresh perspective and ideas.

---

## It all comes down to self-discipline

Getting the balance right between work and you is never easy. And in a world where the pressures of work seem only to increase with every passing year it's tempting (and convenient) to blame the demands of your job for the lack of balance in your work/home life. But the uncomfortable truth is that, contrary to popular opinion, the major tensions that arise because of competing home and work pressures aren't really to do with what kind of job or responsibilities you or your partner has. They're actually more to do with you as a person.

It took me a long time to face up to this. Cornelia, on the other hand, having been married to me for more than twenty years, has few illusions about me. She knows only too well that my workaholic tendencies and other irritating habits have little or nothing to do with what I do for a living. Instead, they're part of *me*. I'd have been every bit as difficult to live with if I'd become a bank manager, plumber, journalist, gardener, milkman or lawyer.

It's uncomfortable to admit it, but the truth is that when we blame 'work' for our failure to give our family the time and support they need, we're deluding ourselves. I'm not trying to dismiss work pressures. I know all too well how real they can be. It's just that going *out* to work doesn't excuse anyone from coming *home* to work.

It's not easy to find time for your family. But then, it's not easy finding the time to mix a passion for work with a passion for swimming, football, squash, bowling, fishing, golf or even the pub, club or gym. In the end it all boils down to willpower and self-discipline. The very undramatic truth is that the decisions *can* be made – if only we're prepared to make them. As they say, 'Where there's a will, there's a way.'

---

**Daphne** (single mum to James, works full time):

When I took on a new job, with a very successful US sales company, I was all too conscious of the heavy work schedule ahead of me. Americans being aware of non-conventional family units meant that I felt able to be more open about my single-parent status. I explained that I'd be able to put 100+ per cent effort into work and I'd need to put an equal amount of effort into my home life. I was also clear about the fact that working on a Sunday was not an option for me. My employers respected both of these areas, which made life much easier at work and at home. That division

---

didn't stop the long hours and commute but it certainly ensured I had 'permission' to try to balance my work and home life.

In the early years with James, it was easier to define 'time for him' as there was feeding, reading, bathing and playing to be done. The teenage years bring a whole new set of requirements as a parent. James is great at letting me wind down from work before unleashing the events from his school day. He doesn't always want to talk but knows that after the wind-down he can have my undivided attention if he needs it.

The challenge for me now is to realise the sort of time that James values with me. I have to listen carefully for pointers. There are times when my just being in the house is sufficient for him; other times he needs to talk and when all else fails and he just wants to enjoy being taller than me I can expect to be thrown, playfully, on the floor and tickled! I look at that as poetic justice and role-reversal, rather than revenge!

## Remember

- Don't beat yourself up about responsibilities you can't shed.
- Avoid blurring the job you do with who you are.
- The childhood years are fleeting – there are only so many conker-collecting days and bonfire nights that your child will want to be with you – so seize the moment.
- The example that you set in balancing your responsibilities will make a marked impact on your child.
- Going out to work doesn't excuse anyone from coming home to work.
- You'll be amazed how many choices you *do* have once you put your mind to it.

## Key principle

**Showing your child that the job you do does not, in itself, define either you as a person or your intrinsic value, is a key responsibility of a parent.**

## How to achieve it

- Work as hard at being a parent as you do at being an employee.
- Give your child your time – in quality *and* quantity.
- Continually prioritise and re-prioritise.
- Don't let work interfere where it doesn't have to.
- Take deliberate steps to have uninterrupted time with your family.
- Don't blame your job for all the hours you work – take responsibility for any workaholic tendencies!

**Top Tip Eight**

# Remember Your Oxygen Mask

Getting the balance right between work and home life isn't easy, but with effort it is just about manageable. However, learning to juggle work and family with finding time for yourself is a trick few of us master. When my own children were young, people used to ask me what I did in my spare time as a hobby. 'Sleep!' was always my answer. For some reason they always laughed, but I was deadly serious. Exhaustion was part and parcel of life as a working parent.

This chapter is all about learning the vital trick of how to juggle that third ball – the all-important task of finding time for yourself before you end up running on empty. So find a little space for yourself right now, sit down with a cup of coffee, and read on!

## First things first

If you have ever travelled on a plane you will know that, just before take-off, one of the cabin staff makes the obligatory announcement about what to do in case of a loss in cabin pressure while other members of the crew stand in the aisles and act out the instructions.

'When the oxygen mask drops down from the compartment above your head, place it over your face, fasten the straps and breathe normally.'

If you are a parent, though, you then get a little extra advice. 'Fasten your own mask before attempting to secure your child's.'

As we all know, most parents' natural instinct would be to help out their child before attempting to take care of themselves. But the airline companies know that trying to fasten an oxygen mask over the head of a frightened and panic-stricken child is difficult and time-consuming. If, at the same time, parents are struggling for breath themselves, the result could well be disastrous for them both.

As you think about your average week, it's vital to put in time for yourself and, if you have one, your partner. The mistake some parents make is to spend virtually every waking moment either working or caring for their child, without creating or protecting a little 'oasis' of time for themselves. As a result, they're almost permanently exhausted, never really feeling they've got on top of things. The irony is, this isn't an efficient way of coping. In fact, it isn't really a way of coping at all.

'Sanity time' is a vital part of any parent's day. But what you actually do to get it will depend on the type of person you are. It may mean relaxing with a glass of wine after the 'human tornado' has gone to bed and you've cleared up the mess. It may mean plonking your child down in front of the TV to watch their favourite video, just to give you half an hour in the middle of the day to regroup and recover your energy. It may mean getting a relative or a good friend to give you an evening off so that you can go out. It may mean taking up a specific interest so your brain (and body) are exercised in doing something constructive that has nothing whatsoever to do with your child. The list is a long one but it's really down to what works for you.

---

**Angela and Stewart** (Angela is at home full time, they have four children, two from Angela's previous relationship)

**Angela**: We try to have a romantic meal once a week so we can have time together, and on Stewart's days off we spend the day together, so sometimes I have to change my diary around to fit in with his shifts. I have a lot of friends I can turn to for a chat.

---

When Henry arrived in Stuttgart to start his new job, he was a bit intimidated by the 'efficiency' of the German workforce. He was dismayed to find that his colleagues arrived for work at 8.30 a.m. and didn't leave until about 8.30 p.m., often taking extra work home with them. The office environment was such that anyone who did less than about a twelve-hour day was considered lazy and inefficient. But with a young family to look after, Henry was determined not to follow their example. Instead, he left work at six, making sure he was back home in time to tuck his two young children into bed and read them a story before spending the rest of the evening with his wife. His colleagues frowned on this early departure, that is until they realised that he *wasn't* lagging behind in terms of his workload. Though he worked ten hours a week less than they did, he seemed to be *more* productive. The reason? He was better motivated and more able to concentrate because he was getting more rest.

Learning to apply the oxygen mask principle in your day-to-day routine will leave you better equipped – physically, mentally and emotionally – to be the parent, and the person, that you and your child want you to be. The principle is: 'Work smarter, not harder.'

---

**Catherine and Paul** (married with three children – Paul works full time, Catherine is on a career break):

**Catherine**: We're very aware of the importance of finding time for ourselves as individuals and as a couple, but it's still something that we find we struggle with practically as we try to organise this into our busy lives with three lively and demanding young children.

I think that we are actually better at finding 'couple time' than individual time. One of the ways we try to do this is by making an effort to eat together every night after the children are in bed and use this time to relax and chat generally about all sorts of things. It's good in one way but does mean we eat late, which is bad for us, and we also know it's something we will have to review as the children get older and stay up later into the evening. We try to make a habit of sitting up to the table as otherwise we slump on the sofa, put the news on and, more often than not, doze off – and before we know it , the evening's gone and we've defeated the whole object of spending time together.

We try to get out together regularly without the children, but despite our best intentions and a willing granny to baby-sit, it doesn't happen as much as we'd like. We have friends who have arranged a regular baby-sitter every other Friday night so that they have at least that quality time together. They say it's made a massive

---

difference to their lives and their marriage. We need to get organised!

We recently arranged for the children to be looked after and I met Paul in the West End to go shopping. It just felt so 'normal' being able to go in and out of shops freely (without visiting the toilet/baby changing area five times an hour) and what luxury to stop at a wine bar for lunch and eat uninterrupted, except by each other! It was a lovely day and we both felt energised and refreshed for days afterwards.

Since I've been at home in the last year, I find it even more difficult to find time to myself than I did when I was at work. At least then I had the journey when I could think or read a book, and a lunch hour (well, sometimes) when I could take a walk and clear my head when I chose to. Now it's non-stop from the moment we wake up to bedtime – I don't resent it, but I am someone who has to find 'space' to survive! I found this the most difficult thing about stopping work and now Titus, our three-year-old, goes to a nursery for a few sessions a week which is good for him and for me! I use the time when he's there for a mixture of 'boring' domestic things but include some 'space', which I sometimes use for things like having my hair cut, phoning or meeting a friend or simply reading a book or a newspaper. It sounds simple, but it makes a world of difference to me and to my attitude to the children at the end of the day.

Recently I had a day out followed by an overnight visit to my sister on my own, which was a lovely break from the routine. I really made the most of it, window-shopped, read, had a manicure even! Paul did a great job of looking after the children, but I did miss them! However, the change made us all appreciate each other much more – I've never had such a welcome home . . . it was great, I might make a habit of it.

## Ask yourself these three questions:

1. **Am I getting enough oxygen at the moment?**

   Every parent would be a martyr if they could. There's something about a child that makes you want to be there for them twenty-four hours a day, seven days a week. Even when you know that being with them is impossible you still feel guilty that you're not there giving them your undivided attention. Combine that with the demands of work and it's almost inevitable that you end up depriving yourself of your own 'air'. But if you really want to succeed as a working parent then a little oxygen for yourself is vital.

2. **Is my relationship with my partner getting enough oxygen?**

   In a culture where the average marriage lasts just nine years, and one in ten cohabiting couples separate within five, it's clear that sustaining a long-term relationship isn't easy. But that doesn't mean it's impossible. No relationship can last, however, if you and your partner don't get the chance to nurture it, to spend time together, to communicate and share your lives. When Cornelia and I first got married, we could go for romantic walks, have evenings to ourselves, lie in the bath for hours, stay out late and plan self-indulgent holidays. Then we had kids! Children are all-consuming, which means you can never regain those carefree days before they arrived. But for the health of your relationship you must work hard to build into your work/life balance some quality time to be together.

3. **Am I feeding enough oxygen to any other vital relationships?**

   While it's vital that you give time to your children and your partner it's also important not to allow the contact you have with your wider circle of family and friends to lapse. The support and strength that these relationships

supply is essential for the long and sometimes difficult work of bringing up your child and not just to surviving – but thriving – through the whole experience.

*If your answer is 'no' to any of these, follow this four-step plan:*

## 1. Get your diary out

Develop the habit of blocking out time in your diary for yourself, for your work, for your child and for your partner. But be realistic. Don't set well-meaning but impossible ideals. Don't make promises to yourself, your child, or anyone else that you can't keep. If you promise yourself an hour in the gym, plus an hour reading with your child and then some quality undivided time with your partner each evening, the likelihood is that your good intentions are doomed to failure from the word go! Running before you can walk will only lead to deep frustration for you and painful disappointment for the people you most wanted to benefit. So make planned, realistic and achievable changes to your lifestyle. You may not be able to shift much about your diary this week, but as for next week and next month that may well be a different matter.

One of the first places to focus your attention is on your employment. It's obvious that you can do little about the normal hours you are required to be at work and that most jobs require some overtime from time to time to get things done. But warning bells should begin to go off if you are regularly being tempted or asked to stay on and work late. This is precious time for you and your child. Of course it is difficult to learn to say 'no', but it's vital nonetheless. And though you might like to think that you are indispensable, don't kid yourself. The reality is that one day you *will* retire, move on or even perhaps be made redundant and someone else *will* take over from you. Though it's important to be both committed to and conscientious about the work you do, remember that it's only one aspect of your life and your boss is not the only person who needs your time. As the famous saying goes, 'No one ever, on their deathbed, said, "I wish I'd spent more time at work."'

It is pointless, however, to free up time in your diary by being ruthless about your working hours if you then end up just frittering them away again. Be careful not to fall into the trap of filling up your newly acquired 'free' time with a thousand and one other responsibilities that will end up causing you just as much stress as doing all those extra hours at work. Create space in your diary that is *just* space. The pace of life in the twenty-first century is fast and frantic. Just because you have 'a space' in your diary doesn't mean that you should let others fill it with their own demands. Having a bit of time, occasionally, to do nothing is exactly what we all need to really thrive. It's amazing how rejuvenating a little peace and quiet can be.

---

**John** (Dad to Pearse, works from home while his wife works abroad):

I think the main use I'd have for the 'oxygen mask' would be to hide my blushes . . . I'm afraid I'm a bit of a softy when it comes to parental duties. I don't get it right all the time, as will be obvious from my bits in other sections of the book, but I do constantly feel guilty about what I don't do well, and feel like I'm 'fire-fighting' a lot of the time. I'm constantly chasing that mythical 'time to myself' or

---

'week where I can just sleep', which I'm sure will allow me to get myself sorted out once and for all. My wife and I often discuss going away for a holiday but we never seem to get round to it . . . and it would seem a bit unfair to go away without our son, since our schedules and the geographical distance between us means that, while he does get quality time with each of us, he doesn't get that much time with both of us together – something we know he really enjoys.

Recently, I've realised that the only way I'm going to get the time I need to organise myself is to deliberately make space for it, and try to turn down the volume on consequent feelings of selfishness and guilt. I'm hopeful that if I can manage this the knock-on effect will be that a more organised lifestyle will have more space for time with my wife, time with my son, and time we can all spend together.

If you are married, or have a partner, sit down and talk about each other's needs. Learn to co-ordinate your diaries in order to give each other a bit of space. All relationships are about give and take. If your sanity relies on getting the opportunity to make the yoga class every Monday evening, or play five-a-side football every Thursday night, then try to accommodate each other so that you can both find the space you need away from the pressures of work and home-life. And remember, if you help to look after your partner's needs then they'll be in much better shape, physically, mentally and emotionally, to help you look after yours.

## 2. Get your address book out

Think about people – parents, other relatives and friends – who may be able to help you get a bit of space from time to time by baby-sitting or childminding for you. And don't forget that while the oxygen mask principle is essentially based on the need for self-preservation, a little bit of give and take might benefit both you and your friends. Many mums and dads find that they can arrange 'baby-sitting swaps' with friends who are in similar situations. Often your best allies are those who know what you are going through, but it will take a bit of organisation to get a system going.

## 3. Get the local paper out

There's more to life than slobbing-out in front of the TV of an evening. Every local paper carries an entertainments section and a quick glance through it or the relevant sections of the *Yellow Pages* or *Thomson Local* will give you all the information you need to begin to pursue those little windows of opportunity to get out, escape the nine-to-five, the nappy-changing for little ones and constant other demands that older children bring. Check out the nearest cinema, restaurants or sports centre or, if you live near to a college, why not even think about some evening (or day) classes?

## 4. Just get out!

Don't forget that some of the best things in life are free. If you want to unwind there's nothing better than a walk or perhaps a gentle run to clear the cobwebs and stress away. If you've gone to all the trouble of reorganising your diary and clearing some space for yourself, you'll want to make the most of it! Even if it's only for a short while, getting out on your own or with your partner will make a big difference. A walk to the nearest pub or simply a wander round the local park will give you time to think, to talk and to relax. It may not seem worthwhile if you can only find twenty-five minutes in your day but it's surprising how little time you really need to feel refreshed and to recharge your batteries.

And while you're out, think about how you can look after yourself in the longer term. Are there other opportunities you are missing? They may not be obvious at first, so finding time to think is vital. Try to make it a habit. Life moves quickly – especially at the speed children grow and develop – so your circumstances and opportunities will change fairly often. Re-assessing regularly will help you not to miss out on making that all-important time for yourself.

---

**Andy and Debbie** (Mum and Dad to Sam – Andy works from home, Debbie is a part-time nurse)

**Debbie**: For the first six months we hardly ever left Samuel with a baby-sitter. This was partly due to the fact that he was breast-fed, but also due to my paranoia. I had no inclination or desire to go out because I was very tired. We had some offers from baby-sitters but

---

I was and still am very fussy about whom I leave Sam with. I prefer people who know Sam very well, or people who have had experience of looking after their own children. I think that until a child can talk and explain how they feel, some people who don't know them won't know what's wrong or what they need when they cry. This is probably a very narrow-minded attitude but I know that I would not enjoy the evening out if I wasn't confident with the person who was looking after Sam. As he has got older it is easier to leave him with people that he knows. Because I was very stressed and anxious about my house becoming out of control (i.e. untidy, dirty) and because no family was available to give me a couple of hours' grace to do my chores and have time out for myself, we decided to put Samuel in nursery for an extra morning. Although I initially felt guilty about this, Sam loves his time at nursery and I love my Wednesday mornings.

**Andy**: I enjoy playing football and I try, at least as often as I can, to escape on a Monday evening for an hour or so. I'm lucky in that working from home also enables friends (who work nearby) to pop in for lunch sometimes.

Once a week we have a regular group of friends round for a meal, which provides a fantastic informal support group and also a great way for us to relax and let off steam.

## Two last tips

1.  Don't try to make too drastic a change at once, as this will only add to your stress. And don't be put off by the number of times you fail to reach your objective or by the length of time it takes to achieve your new lifestyle. Just learn from your mistakes and set new, more realistic goals.
2.  Finding time for yourself is vital, but don't let your newfound enthusiasm for line-dancing, swimming or sky-diving take over your life to the point where your child feels they are competing once more for your time and

attention. Don't throw the baby out with the bath water – so to speak! They *need* you – not just during the 'formative years' of their life, but into their teenage years and beyond. It's a serious investment to make, but one that'll pay huge dividends for both you and for them later in life.

---

**Daphne** (single mum to James, works full time):

This hasn't been too much of an issue for me, although I've rarely spent much time on my own. I lead a busy life at home as well as work and there's never a dull moment. Taking on too much outside of work has been my biggest challenge.

Certainly when James was at junior school I used time wisely. His seven o'clock bedtime meant that I had a whole evening to myself. When he realised, through school friends, that staying up until eight o'clock was possible I had to restrategise. The deal then became that he could read in his room until it was time to sleep. It wasn't a punishment and he knew it was because I needed time to myself. It hasn't taken many years for the tables to turn, with me going to bed first to read and have quiet time!

In the past I didn't like taking holiday for time on my own; I'd rather spend my days off with James. If I could change anything I would have taken a little more time to myself, without him.

Although I have great friends around me I've been particularly bad at asking for help and baby-sitting. In my head I found it difficult to ask because, as a single parent, I felt unable to repay others' kindness. Being part of a baby-sitting circle was certainly out of the question for me.

My own sporting life took a back seat when James was younger, but it was nearly as fulfilling running the school cricket club on a Saturday. Surprisingly it was James who suggested I take up my school-time love of playing hockey. Although it's oxygen mask time for me, it's great that James sometimes joins us for mid-week training sessions.

It would be easy now to think that having a more self-sufficient teenager means I can just do my own thing. Not having felt particularly deprived of time on my own in the past, I certainly have my eyes and ears open to ensure I keep that balance right.

## Remember

- Rest and 'sanity time' are vital – if elusive – parts of a parent's day.
- Everyone relaxes in different ways, so find your own 'oasis' that you can regularly retreat to.
- If you suspect that some aspect of your life requires more oxygen, do something about it – don't put it off.
- Even a little time to relax is better than none.

## Key principle

**If you look after yourself, as well as looking after your child, you will be better equipped physically, emotionally and mentally to be a parent.**

## How to achieve it

- Put time in your diary for yourself – even if it seems a long way off.
- Build a network of family and friends and other parents to help share the load with each other.
- Be realistic about the time you can spend at work, with your child, with your partner and on your interests.

**Top Tip Nine**

# Talk, Talk and Talk Some More

'Learn from the mistakes of others; you won't live long enough to make them all yourself!' once observed a witty Eleanor Roosevelt. That's why, when it comes to succeeding as a working parent, it's good to talk!

Being a mum or dad is a trial-and-error business at the best of times. Life is often unbalanced, unplanned, unpredictable and sometimes downright chaotic. In the end it's as much about improvisation as anything else. Even those who've been doing it for years still have to make most of it up as they go along! So instead of trying to bring up your child as if you were the first person in the world ever to have had one, talk. Talk to your partner, to your family, to friends in similar situations and to others that you trust. Don't wait to discover the pitfalls of parenting the hard way. Be wise enough to learn from the experience of others – what's worked (or not worked!) for them. However, choose those from whom you take advice carefully. Too much information and opinion can be just as bewildering and unhelpful as no guidance at all. But finding two or three wise individuals or couples you can really rely on to give good, clear, supportive advice might just be one of the best investments you ever make. Quality, not quantity, is the name of the game.

**Andy and Debbie** (Mum and Dad to Sam – Andy works from home, Debbie is a part-time nurse)

**Debbie**: I talked to friends who had returned to work and who were in a similar position and aware of some of the issues of juggling home and work. I knew that I didn't want to work full time, particularly after talking to colleagues whose children were in full-time nursery and were learning things about their children's development only at the weekends. I was able to return to work part time and I'm grateful for that. My colleagues were helpful in reminding me not to rush back to work and to take as much time as I needed and to enjoy motherhood as best I could. Hearing stories of colleagues who were forced to return to work after a few months due to their financial situation, and who I had witnessed crying because they felt forced to leave their children too early, made me determined that I would not go back to work too soon. However, I learnt that whenever you do it, it's still hard. When I talked to my dad he was very opposed to Sam going to a nursery, mainly due to his lack of knowledge about them. This caused me stress but perhaps helped me to think about it more and to be sure that it was the right decision.

For most of the time learning from the parenting experience of others is just a casual thing – the gleaning of wisdom from day-to-day conversation. Much of what you need to succeed as a working parent will come from ordinary, everyday, informal encounters with others who are at a similar life-stage or a little further on in their experience and who can easily identify with you and your circumstances. Sometimes, however, a slightly more formal approach is required. That's not to say that every time the balance between work and home life gets difficult you need to rush out and book an appointment on the counsellor's couch, but simply that it really does help to take the time and trouble to build a small network of people who you feel comfortable to ask, from time to time, for their advice, insight and opinion.

As the ancient African proverb puts it, 'It takes a village to raise a child.' In our culture, parents used to chat at the school gate, in the marketplace, or over the garden fence. But now many of us live far more individual, isolated and autonomous lives. We drop the kids off at school without getting out of our cars; out-of-town supermarkets and shopping websites have replaced the marketplace and, sadly, few of us really know our next-door neighbours anymore. The only semblance of real community that still seems to exist is down at the pub, the sports club or the local church. And perhaps that's why so many of us seem to grasp at the chance of building lasting relationships whenever we can. For instance, it's no coincidence that members of antenatal groups often continue to meet long after their babies have been born.

---

**Angela and Stewart** (Angela is at home full time, they have four children, two from Angela's previous relationship)

**Angela**: I find that talking to my friends is very important. My best friend doesn't live nearby, so I talk to her on the phone at least twice a week. Over the past twenty years we have had some arguments over some silly things, but at the end of the day, we are always there to support each other. Our friendship is important – and if we do have any problems we talk about them. I think that having someone you can trust is important, and trust needs to be built up before you can feel comfortable telling someone what is wrong with you and asking for their advice.

---

So if it does takes a community to raise a child, who is part of your child-rearing community? Who can you talk to, and, more importantly, who *should* you be talking to about the needs, aspirations and difficulties of being a working parent?

## 1. Talk to your partner

Life as a working parent can seem a bit like being employed as a plate-spinner in a circus. There is only one way to ensure everyone is happy – keep all the plates spinning by rushing from pole to pole, watching out for any plate that begins to wobble and stopping it from smashing on the ground. The only problem is that the 'plates' you are 'spinning' as a working parent are your job, your child, your family and friends – and that's a non-stop, twenty-four-hours, seven-days-a-week, fifty-two-weeks-a-year responsibility. In fact, it's really no wonder that, from time to time, it's extremely tempting to deliberately let one or more of the plates fall, just to make the overall task a little bit more achievable.

For those of us who are married or have a partner, it's often this relationship that's the easiest 'plate' to neglect. Perhaps it's because we believe that it will somehow keep spinning even if we ignore it and that even if it does end up falling to the ground it will be robust enough not to smash. However, it's vital that the lines of communication between you and your partner are kept open – for your sake, for their sake and vitally for the sake of your child.

THANKS –
BEING A
WORKING DAD
CAN BE SO
DISTRACTING..
TALKING
TO ANOTHER
PARENT
HELPS.

Hey, WE'VE
BEEN MARRIED
TWO YEARS...
IF WE'RE TALKING
IT'S ABOUT
TIME!

While there are thousands of capable, caring and committed single mums and dads successfully bringing up their children, it remains true that 'two heads are better than one'. So when decisions have to be made and options considered about childcare, schooling, work, etc., the first port of call should be your partner, if you have one. That's not to pretend that talking is always easy. The huge popularity of books, such as *Men Are from Mars, Women Are from Venus*, which have helped many of us fathom the mysteries of gender relationship problems, are ample evidence of that.

So set time aside when you can really talk. 'Pass the TV guide, darling,' isn't communicating. You'll be amazed just how much time you can find if you can resist the temptation to switch on the television every evening and vegetate in front of it with glazed eyes. What you need together is uninterrupted and undistracted time. Why not book it into your diary if that's the only way to make it happen? If you are going to get beyond the superficial pleasantries of 'Did you have a good day at the office?' then you are going to have to work to make it happen. Getting beyond the generalities and the practicalities of day-to-day living will take more than a few minutes of tired conversation at the end of a long day.

Once you have found the space and time to talk, don't be afraid to be honest about any issues that are worrying you. Ignoring them won't make them go away. Instead they will just fester away until they are dealt with. So be good to yourself and deal with them now! Be honest about your expectations of one another as parents. Talk about the issues you are facing, the questions that you have, the way you are feeling, and practical ways of moving forward. And don't just talk – actively listen to one another. Good communication only occurs when you are just as open to listening as you are to talking. It is now widely recognised that, besides the practical direction it offers, the simple act of talking and being listened to is, in itself, one of the most beneficial ways to relieve stress and anxiety.

**John** (Dad to Pearse, works from home while his wife works abroad):

I talk to Pearse constantly, of course, and even more so as he gets older. For instance, we have a lot of the same favourite TV shows and movies, probably due to me being about twelve mentally... What's going to happen when Pearse gets to thirteen and is telling me to switch off the cartoons so he can watch a news show?

My wife and I talk a lot on the phone too, especially when she's away. In fact we sometimes think we probably talk more than working couples who actually live together and only have snatched conversation during the breakfast rush or just before they fall asleep exhausted.

But the biggest revelation for me in terms of talking has been talking with other parents, whether at church or at the school gate, or engaging work colleagues who have kids themselves in conversations about how they manage. In the high-pressure worlds of media and TV where I work I've been surprised to find that kids are the great leveller – from big celebrities to hard-bitten journalists and producers you often only have to mention the subject of kids and the floodgates open. I guess we all have concerns and guilt about the work/parenting balance and completely separate from the tips that can be shared, there's just a lot of comfort in knowing that every other working parent shares the same concerns. One of the biggest obstacles to being a good parent is trying to carry the weight of being that mythical 'perfect' parent.

## 2. Talk to people who are in the same situation as you

The next time you are on the school run vying for a parking space with all those other stressed-out, rushed-off-their-feet mothers and fathers, remind yourself that many of them are going through exactly what you are going through. And more importantly, just like you, may well be wishing they had someone to talk to, to share their experiences with and pick up a bit of wisdom from. So why not take the opportunity to introduce yourself to a few of them?

If you can't find the time to get to know the parents of children who attend the same school as your child, why not chat to a colleague at work with children the same age as yours, or seek out the opportunity to talk to the other mums and dads if your child belongs to a club like the Cubs or Scouts, Brownies or Girl Guides, or a dance or football club? Parents who are in similar situations to you can often prove to be a goldmine of reassurance and practical help. Be honest about the trials and tribulations you are facing as a working parent. Find out what does or doesn't work for them. And, of course, there's no reason why it should be one-way traffic. They are bound to appreciate your honesty, and your experiences, insights and ideas will help them every little bit as much as theirs will help you.

An honest, independent view of your situation and the options facing you can be a huge help when it comes to distinguishing the wood from the trees, and may provide you with genuine alternatives for solving particular problems. Talking to others will also remind you that you're not on your own, however isolated you may feel at times. At a deeper level, too, it can be very reassuring when you hear others confirm that they think you're doing a good job and that you've got the balance right. It is not without reason that they say, 'A problem shared is a problem halved.'

Rather than feeling that we know it all now, the longer we are parents, the more we feel that we need others – family members, friends, work colleagues – to help us out both with advice about our children and in practical ways. If we share things with those we trust and respect then we, and our children, stand to gain a lot from their experience and expertise, and if we don't then it's likely that we'll be the losers.

**Paul and Catherine** (married with three children – Paul works full time, Catherine is on a career break)

**Catherine**: When we first became parents, we were quite reluctant to talk to other people about 'parenting' things. Some we'd chatted to during pregnancy had been so negative – we were fed up of hearing about 'sleepless nights' and 'things will never be the same again' that we felt we were better off getting through most things together, apart from advice from professionals like doctors or health visitors. We did compare notes with others in our NCT (National Childbirth Trust) class at the beginning, but after I went back to work there wasn't much time for keeping up those contacts regularly.

At work, I was the only person in my area who'd had a baby, so I didn't have anyone there to chat to about work/home balance. It was a pressurised environment and I spent most of my time denying that being a mum made any difference to my working life at all! Looking back, there must have been lots of women in other departments who I could have linked up with, but I don't remember having the time to seek them out. I was quite isolated in that respect really.

When I returned to work after our second baby, things had changed a lot in a short time, and so had we! I got to know several people at work with children including my mentor and found this a real help. Grace, our baby daughter, had bad colic and didn't sleep well – I was happy to talk to other people and really grateful for advice from friends offering tips on managing colic, latest theories on sleep or calming down strategies for us and our baby!

It was through chatting with a work-colleague mum that we found we had a lot in common and our job-share was 'born'. Talking things through with two other women who had done the same thing successfully at a senior level was invaluable, and their advice helped us shape the way we would work together.

Once I was working part time and Luke was at nursery and later at school, I suddenly discovered a wealth of free advice and support at the school gate. But there is such a thing as too much good advice and I've had to learn to distinguish genuinely helpful information from people wanting to tell you their opinions on how to raise your child and run your life!

We've found it's really good to talk to other working parents and see how they managed the demands of work and home – it's very reassuring to compare notes, share things and find that you're not on your own. When our nanny left, it was through chatting to others that we found a brilliant childminder who was able at very short notice to look after all three children until I stopped work. If I hadn't shared our 'crisis', I don't know what we would have done.

Paul especially values chatting to other dads we know on trying to juggle work and home life as well as getting and handing on tips on coping with all the other demands of being a dad of three.

## 3. Talk to people who are in a different situation from yours

As well as talking to your partner and to other parents in similar situations to yours, talk to older, respected friends, who have faced the work/life balance issues some time ago. The likelihood is that, if they know you well, they will be able to provide some incredibly valuable and objective insight into your situation.

One couple I know were having big problems with their teenage son and daughter. They felt that they had simply run out of ideas and energy. As a last resort, they decided to take the rather drastic step of inviting two of their most respected and trusted friends (who were a few years older than them) to live with them for a week. The idea was simple. They asked them to watch the way that the house operated and then to be honest with them about what they saw. Their children were none the wiser – it was a fairly regular occurrence for them to have people staying, so family life went on as normal.

On the Friday night at the end of the week the couple took their friends out for a meal and spent the evening asking for honest feedback on their parenting 'style'. They listened carefully to what their friends had to say – both the encouraging and the not-so-encouraging insights. The next evening, having had the chance to absorb their friends' input and think things over, they sat down over a bottle of wine and talked about the changes that they felt they needed to make for the future. Over ten years later they still maintain that it was one of the most valuable things they have ever done as parents.

## No pain, no gain

You might not want to go quite as far as my friends, but the idea behind what they did has to be a principle well worth thinking about.

> **Daphne** (single mum to James, works full time):
>
> Being a working parent has just been part of life for me. The fact that I'm on my own means decision-making can be a lonely process. I have a few close friends with whom I can share most things and ideas without feeling embarrassed or stupid. I've learnt, too late in James' life, to talk about things with others and wish I'd shared ideas and challenges before now. As it is, with another imminent

change in the way I balance work and home, I'm definitely going to take the opportunity of brainstorming with some carefully chosen friends.

It's not just other parents and friends I need to talk to. It's all too easy to pigeonhole children, particularly teenagers, into the current stereotype and ignore their views. James needs to be included in my thought process so he can try to understand what's going on. It wouldn't be appropriate to burden him with the nitty-gritty, and what self-respecting teenager would want to admit they'd like to see their parents more often? Nonetheless, he and I are very close and to ignore him in this sort of discussion would be the opposite of our normal behaviour. How on earth do I go about having that sort of conversation in competition with the Game Cube and TV? I've found in the past that listening is more important than talking. If I go for the 'big, serious chat' he automatically thinks my soapbox is going to make an appearance or he's done something wrong and so closes down completely. I find that washing-up time is neutral ground, with not much eye contact – it works well. Also, not taking myself too seriously. Fragmented comments over the course of a weekend start to form an overall picture that can be helpful.

Seeking advice from others takes courage and often comes at a cost – especially if you are asking them to be honest with you – but it's surely a price worth paying if it means you and your child benefit from it. Being a parent, especially a working parent, is one of the biggest challenges – as well as privileges – that you will ever face. At work we all rely on the feedback, informal and formal (reviews and appraisals), of our colleagues and managers in order to grow and develop, to build on our strengths and to recognise our weaknesses. To fail to take advantage of the insights of others leaves us weaker, not stronger. The reality is that, in the same way, so much of your success as a working parent will come down to the simple act of talking openly about your situation to others whom you trust and respect and giving them the opportunity to be honest with you. And though it will be a painful experience at times, you will also discover it to be a liberating one. As the BT advert used to remind us, it really is 'good to talk'.

## Remember

- It really does take a village to raise a child, so it's only wise to talk to other people.
- You are not the first person in the world to be a parent, so don't wait to discover all the pitfalls for yourself!
- Be selective about the people from whom you ask advice, but don't just ask people who will give you the answers that you want to hear.
- Go for quality, not quantity, of information.
- Work hard to communicate with those people who are closest to you.

## Key principle

**Talk to other people whom you trust and respect (and who know you) about your life as a parent. Listen to what they have to say.**

## How to achieve it

- Choose family and friends that you trust to talk to.
- Talk about the hard issues as well as the success stories.
- Don't do all the talking – listen as well.
- Talk to people who are in the same situation as you.
- Talk to people who have already 'been there' and faced your situation.

# Reassess Regularly

I've got a confession to make. Ever since my boyhood I've been a supporter of Crystal Palace Football Club. Which, I'm sure you realise, means that I have had to learn to cope with the inevitable stream of hard-to-bear jokes that go with such a commitment. This situation is due, of course, to the Eagles' consistently patchy performance and the resulting annual promotion/relegation struggle. (A Palace supporter rings up to ask the time of Saturday's kick-off. 'When can you get there?' comes the response, 'And – can you bring your kit?' The list goes on.)

But even as a Palace supporter I have learned that football is about strategy as well as talent. A season is made up of well over forty games, which means that success for any manager is about planning for the long haul by constantly reassessing their situation and opportunities. That means that a wise manager won't necessarily use all his best players in every game; he won't choose to play every game at the same pace; he won't always use the same team or the same team shape; he will adapt his tactics depending on the way that their opponents are performing; and he may choose to make substitutions early or late in the game, or not at all. What's more, I know that constant reappraisal is vital not just because Palace is Palace, but because every team from Manchester United to Barnet and Liverpool to Hull City does exactly the same. In fact, the more successful the team, the more intense is the pursuit of excellence, and the more rigorous is the commitment to constant re-evaluation.

**Catherine and Paul** (married with three children – Paul works full time, Catherine is on a career break)

**Catherine**: One thing we've learned since having our first child nearly ten years ago is the art of tackling life as in 'bite-sized' pieces! We find that when you try to plan a great chunk of your life (whether home or work life) at once and set your heart on continuing along a particular course, you'll almost certainly find things change, and disrupt the master plan.

Things are more unpredictable once you become parents, and any change has bigger implications once you are a family. For us, changing jobs, moving house, nannies leaving, children going to school and having a new baby have obviously come with a fair amount of stress along the way, but we find it's easier to cope with all these things when we take a more flexible attitude to planning ahead and try a bit more to take things as they come.

We've also found these times provide natural opportunities to reassess and to change other things in our lives that might help our family life jog along a little bit easier. The alternative – kicking against change and continuing regardless – has usually been a recipe for unhappiness all round.

There have been times when we haven't taken the time to look seriously at our family's changing needs – especially after the birth of our second child. It was almost certainly one of the most chaotic periods in our lives: we had a toddler and an unsettled baby; we were moving into a wreck of a house with immediate work to be done; I was returning to work to a new job; we had a new nanny starting (all within the space of a month); and money was tight! We must have been mad.

The bad timing was unavoidable as we'd had so many delays in our move, which weren't our fault. But we could have taken a step back then, and looked at better ways of getting through that difficult time. I could have possibly delayed my start back at work if we'd budgeted better during my maternity leave; maybe I could have negotiated going back part time for a while; or perhaps we should have gone to stay with family for a month or two until things had settled down! Everything worked out in the end, but it was very stressful and the children must have suffered through our utter exhaustion and frustration. A little bit of time taken to size up the situation in advance would have paid dividends.

After this experience, we made some quite radical changes and I went part time, job-sharing, which made a tremendous difference to everyone. It was also a time for reassessment for Paul who changed jobs – which turned out to be a very positive move in the longer term.

We've had to reassess our childcare needs often, after the birth of each child and as they get older. Full days at nursery were a great option with one toddler but when number two came along it didn't work as the nursery didn't take babies and Luke was due to start school nursery anyway. We found a solution by employing a nanny who could care for Grace at home and take and collect Luke from nursery each day. Likewise, having planned childcare carefully after the birth of our third baby, we found that in reality the arrangement didn't work so we had to look at things again. On the whole, changes we've had to make have worked out for the better.

Now our children are getting older we find we can involve them in discussions about how things are going. That way, we can tackle issues when they come up and plan any changes calmly before they become problems and we're in a panic. Our next challenge will be to look at what happens next year when I plan to return to work after a break – the reassessment starts now!

'The road to success,' it has been said, 'is always under construction.' Put another way, the rule is, 'Never rest on your laurels.' Continuous reassessment is essential in order to maintain progress and growth. Yesterday's success is no guarantee for tomorrow's. There is no such thing as 'business as usual'! As one business guru put it, 'Even if you're on the right track, you'll still get run over if all you do is sit on it.'

Life has a habit of changing course just when you think you've got things all sorted. From sport to computing, music to healthcare, fashion to politics, education to communications, change is the only thing that you can really rely on in life. And the truth is that parenting is no different.

**Angela and Stewart** (Angela is at home full time, they have four children, two from Angela's previous relationship)

**Angela**: We've learnt a lot over the years. We've learnt a lot through the problems we had when James, the oldest, was growing up, and have put this into practice with the girls.

Just because two of the girls are disabled doesn't mean we have to wrap them up in cotton wool. We try always to have a listening ear and not to take sides. We try to present a united front on any subject. We've also made it a priority to spend time with the children at least twice a week.

We've learnt to show love as well as authority when we tell them off. As he works shifts, Stewart is sometimes at home in the morning, sometimes in the afternoon and sometimes at night, so the children do see him and he can help out.

One thing that we've found really important is to be honest – when we have to talk to the children about a subject we are honest to them about how we really feel.

There have been moments when as a parent I've been tempted to think that I've got it all sewn up, but then I've arrived home! There are times when every parent feels that they've got it mastered, that their work/home balance is working well and that life is running smoothly. But being a working parent is rather like playing a game of snakes and ladders. One moment you are forging ahead, climbing the ladder of success but then, just when you think you've got it made, another little snake raises its ugly head and you find yourself sliding right back to where you started, or even worse!

Even if you have read, digested and implemented every word and suggestion in this book, there's still no time to sit back and relax. Your continued success as a working parent is quite simply dependent on your ability and willingness to constantly reassess, re-evaluate, adapt and change your priorities and practices as your child grows. What may have been a fantastic arrangement a year ago may not be so suitable now. A bedtime 'Thomas the Tank Engine' story, a cup of hot chocolate and a goodnight kiss when I get in from work doesn't go down quite as well now with my eighteen-year-old son as it used to.

DO WE NEED TO REASSESS THE TIME WE SPEND WITH OUR KIDS NOW THAT THEY'RE TEENAGERS?

THEY'RE TEENAGERS?! WHEN DID THAT HAPPEN?

**Daphne** (single mum to James, works full time):

With life running along at full pelt, a child to feed, a home to run, bills to pay and a million other things on the go, seeing the wood for the trees has to be one of the most difficult issues of all for me. Change is happening all around me in the shape of James growing up, moving schools, meeting new friends and becoming smarter at pushing the boundaries as he learns about life.

Children love a routine and, hopefully, they grow faster than their parents. It's been important for me to constantly reassess our routines to realise what is appropriate. Meandering to school hand in hand with his mother was never going to work for James at twelve years old; but starting the day and catching the train together is an option that has suited us both.

After eleven years of having a live-in nanny it was a huge shock to be 'home alone' with James. It was a shock even though we'd planned it for about six months and I'd known, since her arrival, that Rachel couldn't be with us forever.

It's taken me a while to learn to pre-empt changes but now I'm on the lookout for them. Once I can accept change I can learn to do something positive about it and relish the outcome. Change doesn't always need to be dramatic; little things like introducing a new routine at breakfast can make a big improvement in communication. The smell of cooking sausages (weekends only) invariably brings James downstairs, giving us an opportunity to at least grunt at one another before the day begins.

> Reassessing James' needs must go hand in hand with working out my needs. One of my goals is for neither of us to end up bitter and twisted about bad or miscalculated decisions.

The trouble is, taking time to reassess does exactly what it says – it takes time. And in the busyness of life, it's more than tempting to 'sweep things under the carpet'. The truth is that, however inviting, this is always a false economy. We all know that it makes much better sense to keep one step ahead of the game and set aside an hour or two, every few months, just to consciously check how things are going and to address issues before they become acute problems. Ask yourself questions like:

- Am I content that my current arrangements are still the best for me, my child and our life together?
- Have my working hours or salary changed?
- Do I need more or less hours of childcare?
- Am I able to spend the time with my child that I promised?
- Are things working out the way that I planned or have they slipped a bit?

**John** (Dad to Pearse, works from home while his wife works abroad):

Now that Pearse is in his second year at 'big school', an area I'm having to constantly reassess is the time taken to do his homework. At seven, he still needs to be supervised and helped while doing it, but since he's now got a lot more to do over a wider range of subjects the old system of taking a specific night during the week doesn't work anymore. It's more practical to take a little time every night and do a bit so it all gets done by the weekend. The challenge is making sure it all does get done and on the right day – like his dad before him, Pearse likes to tackle the subjects he enjoys first, and leave the rest on the long finger.

In this particular area of parenting, reassessing is relatively easy – liaison with teachers and checking comments in Pearse's homework tells me how we're doing. But one thing I have learned is that the nature of reassessment is you don't always get it right the first, second or even third time. It's important to accept that there will be hiccups along the way, and if the first few assessments point out that some area is no longer working, keep adjusting and readjusting until you both find a way that does work.

A regular and honest evaluation will probably not turn out to be half as painful as you might think, but it will provide you with the opportunity you need to make changes for the better. And, if your goal is to build a strong, loving and committed relationship with your child, then it's essential.

For all of us, there will be those occasions when reassessment will mean major upheaval; while at other times it will bring no more than minor adjustments at the margins. But, however marginal or far-reaching, both you and your child will, in the long run, be thankful that you invested the time to think about the way ahead.

**Andy and Debbie** (Mum and Dad to Sam – Andy works from home, Debbie is a part-time nurse)

**Debbie**: There was a point where I wasn't coping, while being at home with Sam more than being at work. I was also offered an opportunity for promotion. This required a review of the situation and careful thought as to the consequences for Sam, Andy and myself if I was to work more hours. At the time, I didn't like being at home on my own (as I'm a people person) and felt that I would get more satisfaction from work colleagues and tackling new problems at work than going for the daily walk to the park with Sam and the dog. After a few weeks thinking and mulling over the options I decided to continue in my current role, working two days a week. As Samuel has started to talk he has become a little person who's happy to help Mummy with everything! He is now good company and I would have missed out on this lovely stage if I had increased my hours. However, I have learnt that I need to meet with others and socialise frequently, and that takes effort.

'Be good to your child,' I once heard a comedian wryly suggest, 'because they will get to choose your nursing home!' A funny line, but like all comedy, built around at least a hint of truth. The reality is that when the business decisions, the deadlines and the deals that so concern and consume you now are not only history but, for the most part, completely forgotten, when the names and faces of some of the colleagues you worked with are no more than distant memories, the thing that will still bring you joy is a good relationship with your child and, maybe by then, their children as well. So get wise. Invest in the future today and make the 'parent' part of 'working parent' a priority for you.

## Remember

- Encountering problems rarely means having to start all over again. Issues that create stress for you in your work/family balance can often be overcome by an honest evaluation and some smaller changes at the margins.
- It's much better to keep one step ahead of the game than constantly respond to crises.
- Regularly reviewing your family's circumstances is a useful aid to communication.
- As they get older, involve your child in the decisions that you make which have a bearing on them.

## Key principle

**As circumstances change and your children grow up, it's wise to take a fresh look at things once in a while.**

## How to achieve it

- Regularly reassess and re-evaluate your situation, changing your priorities as your child grows.
- Ask yourself, your child and your partner how they feel things are working out.
- Don't be afraid to get an external perspective from someone you trust.
- Be committed to making changes where necessary – your family will thank you for it.

# Further Information

## Organisations

### Parentalk
PO Box 23142
London SE1 OZT

Tel: 020 7450 9073
Fax: 020 7450 9060
e-mail: info@parentalk.co.uk
Website: www.parentalk.co.uk

*Provides a range of resources and services designed to inspire
parents to enjoy parenthood.*

### BBC Website
Website: www.bbc.co.uk/health/parenting

*Gives advice on parenting, preparing for parenthood throughout
the pregnancy, illnesses, your baby's needs and your needs.
Produced in collaboration with the Health Education Authority
(now the Health Development Agency – www.ohn.gov.uk).*

### Care for the Family
PO Box 488
Cardiff CF15 7YY

Tel: 029 2081 0800
Fax: 029 2081 4089
e-mail: mail@cff.org.uk
Website: www.care-for-the-family.org.uk

*Provides support for families through seminars, resources and
special projects.*

## Chartered Institute of Personnel Development
Website: www.ipd.co.uk

*This organisation provides, among other things, help with employment law. For this, click into the section 'Confused about employment law'.*

## Child Benefit Centre
Department for Work and Pensions
Child Benefit Centre (Washington)
PO Box 1
Newcastle-upon-Tyne NE88 1AA

Tel: 0870 155 5540
e-mail: child-benefit@dwp.gsi.gov.uk
Website: www.dwp.gov.uk

*Administers all child benefits claims.*

## Childcare Link
Trust Court
Vision Park
Histon
Cambridge CB4 9PW

Helpline: 0800 096 0296
Website: www.childcarelink.gov.uk

## Child Support Agency
PO Box 55
Brierley Hill
West Midlands DY5 1YL

Tel: 08457 133133 (enquiry line)/08457 138924 (for those who are hard of hearing)
e-mail: csa-net@dwp.gsi.gov.uk
Website: www.dss.gov.uk/csa

*In Northern Ireland:*
Great Northern Tower
17 Great Victoria Street
Belfast BT2 7AD

Tel: 08457 132000
e-mail: belfast-cust-helpline@dwp.gsi.gov.uk

*The Government agency that assesses maintenance levels for parents who no longer live with their children.*

## Childalert
e-mail: info@childalert.co.uk
Website: www.childalert.co.uk

*Childalert is an information service for parents and anyone else looking after children. It provides information about child safety and wellbeing in the home and on the move, covering pre-conception to the first weeks at home, to the energy and determination of toddlers, to the concerns of raising boys and girls and how different they can be.*

## Children 1st
83 Whitehouse Loan
Edinburgh EH9 1AT

Tel: 0131 446 2300
Fax: 0131 446 2339
e-mail: info@children1st.org.uk
Website: www.children1st.org.uk

*A national Scottish voluntary organisation providing advice and support to parents on the care and protection of their children.*

## Citizens' Advice Bureau (CAB)
Website: www.nacab.org.uk/

*A free and confidential service giving information and advice on topics such as benefits; maternity rights; debts; housing, consumer, employment and legal problems; family and personal difficulties. It also has details of useful national and local organisations. Ask at your local library or look in your phone book for your nearest office. Opening times may vary.*

## Couple Counselling Scotland
18 York Place
Edinburgh EH1 3EP

Tel: 0131 558 9669
Fax: 0131 556 6596
e-mail: enquiries@couplecounselling.org
Website: www.couplecounselling.org

*Provides a confidential counselling service for relationship problems of any kind.*

## Credit Action
6 Regent Terrace
Cambridge CB2 1AA

Helpline: 0800 591084
Tel: 01223 324034
e-mail: office@creditaction.com
Website: www.creditaction.com

*The National Money Education Charity that promotes self-help in money education matters. Practical, sensitive and confidential advice on debt management is available via the freephone helpline. Also, a free self-help guide will be sent where appropriate. The money guide section has a good self-help guide to dealing with personal debt.*

## Daycare Trust
21 St George's Road
London SE1 6ES

Tel: 020 7840 3350
e-mail: info@daycaretrust.org.uk
Website: www.daycaretrust.org.uk

*Gives free advice to parents on childcare issues, promotes affordable childcare and helps you to decide what type of childcare might suit your child and family circumstances.*

## Department for Work and Pensions

Correspondence Unit, Room 540
The Adelphi
1–11 John Adam Street
London WC2N 6HT

Tel: 020 7712 2171 (Mon–Fri 9 a.m.–5 p.m.)
Fax: 020 7712 2386
Website: www.dwp.gov.uk

*DWP was formed from the Department of Social Security and the former Department of Education and Employment. The Department is responsible for delivering support and advice through a modern network of services to people of working age, employers, pensioners, families and children, and disabled people. Its key aims are to help customers become financially independent and to help reduce child poverty.*

## Department of Trade and Industry

DTI Enquiry Unit
1 Victoria Street
London SW1H 0ET

Tel: 020 7215 5000
e-mail: enquiries@dti.gsi.gov.uk
Website: www.dti.gov.uk

## Work-Life Balance Team

Address as above

Tel: 020 7215 6249
E-mail: team.work-life-balance@dti.gsi.gov.uk
Website: www.dti.gov.uk/work-lifebalance

Also look at:

www.tiger.gov.uk *(an interactive website for you to calculate your maternity leave and follow new developments)*

*The DTI publications 'Parental Leave: A Short Guide', 'Time Off for Dependents: A Short Guide', 'Maternity Rights: A Short Guide' and 'Partnerships with People' are available free.*

## Employers for Work-Life Balance

Celcon House
289–293 High Holborn
London WC1V 7HU
e-mail: secretariat@wfdeurope.com
Website: www.employersforwork-lifebalance.org.uk

*Aims to share best practices and demonstrate to large and small employers how work-life policies can be introduced on a practical basis.*

## Equality Direct

Advice line: 0845 600 34444
Website: www.equalitydirect.org.uk

*Offers advice for businesses on equality issues such as flexible working.*

## Fathers Direct

Herald House
Lambs Passage
Bunhill Row
London EC1Y 8TQ

Tel: 020 7920 9491
Fax: 020 7374 2966
e-mail: enquiries@fathersdirect.com
Website: www.fathersdirect.com

*An information resource for fathers.*

## Flexecutive
Shropshire House
179 Tottenham Court Road
London W1T 7NZ

Tel: 020 7636 6744
e-mail: admin@flexecutive.co.uk
Website: www.flexecutive.co.uk

*Are experts in the field of flexible work for professionals looking to balance their work and personal life. Operates nationwide.*

## Gingerbread
7 Sovereign Close
Sovereign Court
London E1W 3HW

Advice line: 0800 018 4318 (Mon–Fri 9 a.m.–5 p.m.)
Tel: 020 7488 9300
Fax: 020 7488 9333
e-mail: office@gingerbread.org.uk
Website: www.gingerbread.org.uk

*Provides day-to-day support and practical help for lone parents.*

## Health Development Agency
Holborn Gate
330 High Holborn
London WC1 7BA

Tel: 020 7430 0850
Publications line: 01235 465565
Fax: 020 7061 3390
e-mail: communications@had-online.org.uk
Website: www.had-online.org.uk

*Produces a wide range of leaflets and other useful information for families on a wide variety of topics.*

## Home-Start UK
2 Salisbury Road
Leicester LE1 7QR

Tel: 0116 233 9955
Fax: 0116 233 0232
e-mail: info@home-start.org.uk
Website: www.home-start.org.uk

## Homeworking.com
c/o Knowledge Computing
9 Ashdown Drive
Borehamwood
Herts WD6 4LZ

Fax: 0870 284 8769
e-mail: admin@homeworking.com
Website: www.homeworking.com

*A useful site for anyone wanting to work at home or already doing so.*

## Kids Club Network
Bellerive House
3 Muirfield Crescent
London E14 9SZ

Tel: 020 7512 2100
Website: www.kidsclubs.com

*Offers information and advice on out-of-school childcare.*

## Maternity Alliance
2–6 Northburgh Street
London EC1V 0AY

Tel: 020 7490 7639
Information line: 020 7490 7638

e-mail: info@maternityalliance.org.uk
Website: www.maternityalliance.org.uk

*Supports pregnant women and parents-to-be.*

## National Childminding Association
8 Masons Hill
Bromley
Kent BR2 9EY

Advice line: 0800 169 4486 (Mon, Tues & Thurs 10 a.m.–12 & 2–4 p.m.; Fri 2–4 p.m.)
Tel: 020 8464 6164
Fax: 020 8290 6834
e-mail: info@ncma.org.uk
Website: www.ncma.org.uk

*Informs childminders, parents and employers about the best practices in childminding.*

## National Council for One Parent Families
255 Kentish Town Road
London NW5 2LX

Lone Parent Line: 0800 018 5026 (Mon–Fri 9.15 a.m.–5.15 p.m.)
Advice on maintenance benefits and money issues is available on the helpline Mon & Thurs 11 a.m.–2 p.m.; Tues 3–6 p.m.
General enquiries: 020 7428 5400
Fax: 020 7482 4851
e-mail: info@oneparentfamilies.org.uk
Website: www.oneparentfamilies.org.uk

*An information service for lone parents.*

## National Family and Parenting Institute

430 Highgate Studios
53–79 Highgate Road
London NW5 1TL

Tel: 020 7424 3460
Fax: 020 7485 3590
e-mail: info@nfpi.org
Website: www.nfpi.org

*An independent charity set up to provide a strong national focus on parenting and families in the twenty-first century.*

## National NEWPIN (New Parent and Infant Network)

Sutherland House
35 Sutherland Square
Walworth
London SE17 3EE

Tel: 020 7358 5900
Fax: 020 7701 2660
e-mail: info@newpin.org.uk
Website: www.newpin.org.uk

*A network of local centres offering a range of services for parents and children.*

## National Work-Life Forum

c/o The Industrial Society
48 Bryanston Square
London SW1E 6HF

Tel: 020 7479 2141
Website: www.worklifeforum.com

*Provides advice for employers on work-life issues.*

## New Ways to Work
26 Shacklewell Lane
Dalston
London E8 2EZ

Tel: 020 7503 3283
e-mail: information@new-ways.co.uk
Website: www.new-ways.co.uk

*Gives information and advice on working arrangements, and publishes useful publications.*

## NHS Direct
Advice line: 0845 4647
Website: www.nhsdirect.co.uk

## NIPPA (The early years organisation)
6C Wildflower Way
Apollo Road
Belfast BT12 6TA

Tel: 028 9066 2825
Fax: 028 9038 1270
e-mail: mail@nippa.org
Website: www.nippa.org

*Promotes high-quality early childhood care and education services.*

## NSPCC
Weston House
42 Curtain Road
London EC2A 3NH

Helpline: 0800 800 5000
Tel: 020 7825 2500
Fax: 020 7825 2525
Website: www.nspcc.org.uk

*Aims to prevent child abuse and neglect in all its forms and give practical help to families with children at risk. The NSPCC also produces leaflets with information and advice on positive parenting – for these, call 020 7825 2500.*

## One Parent Families Scotland
13 Gayfield Square
Edinburgh EH1 3NX

Tel: 0131 556 3899
Fax: 0131 557 7899
e-mail: info@opfs.org.uk
Website: www.opfs.org.uk

*Provides information, training, counselling and support to one-parent families throughout Scotland.*

## Oneplusone
The Wells
7/15 Rosebery Avenue
London EC1R 4SP

Tel: 020 7841 3660
Fax: 020 7841 3670
e-mail: info@oneplusone.org.uk
Website: www.oneplusone.org.uk

*Aims to build through research a framework for understanding contemporary marriage and partnership.*

## Parenting Education and Support Forum
Unit 431 Highgate Studios
53–79 Highgate Road
London NW5 1TL

Tel: 020 7284 8370
Fax: 020 7485 3587
e-mail: pesf@dial.pipex.com
Website: www.parenting-forum.org.uk

*Aims to raise awareness of the importance of parenting and its impact on all aspects of child development.*

## Parentline Plus

520 Highgate Studios
53–76 Highgate Road
Kentish Town
London NW5 1TL

Helpline: 0808 800 2222
Textphone: 0800 783 6783
Fax: 020 7284 5501
e-mail: centraloffice@parentlineplus.org.uk
Website: www.parentlineplus.org.uk

*Provides a freephone helpline called Parentline and courses for parents via the Parent Network Service. Parentline Plus also includes the National Stepfamily Association. For all information, call the Parentline freephone number: 0808 800 2222.*

## Parents Advice Centre

Floor 4, Franklin House
12 Brunswick Street
Belfast BT2 7GE

Helpline: 028 9023 8800
Tel: 028 9031 0891
Fax: 028 9031 2475
e-mail: belfast@pachelp.org
Website: www.pachelp.org

*A voluntary organisation that offers support, guidance and counselling to parents and young people with family difficulties.*

## Parents at Work
1/3 Berry Street
London EC1V 0AA

Tel: 020 7628 3565
Fax: 020 7628 3591
e-mail: info@parentsatwork.org.uk
Website: www.parentsatwork.org.uk

*By working with parents and organisations alike, Parents at Work helps children, working parents and their emplotyers to find a better balance between responsibilities at home and work.*

## Positive Parenting
1st Floor
2A South Street
Gosport PO12 1ES

Tel: 023 9252 8787
Fax: 023 9250 1111
e-mail: info@parenting.org.uk
Website: www.parenting.org.uk

*Aims to prepare people for the role of parenting by helping parents, those about to become parents and also those who lead parenting groups.*

## Pre-School Learning Alliance
69 Kings Cross Road
London WC1X 9LL

Tel: 020 7833 0991
Fax: 020 7837 4942
e-mail: pla@pre-school.org.uk
Website: www.pre-school.org.uk

*An educational charity that represents and supports community pre-schools in England.*

# raisingkids.co.uk
Website: www.raisingkids.co.uk

*This website provides individual advice from Dr Pat Spungin and other qualified experts, a huge reference library of parenting solutions, plus online discussions for support from the raisingkids.co.uk online community of parents in similar situations.*

# Relate
Herbert Gray College
Little Church Street
Rugby CV21 3AP

Helpline: 0845 130 4010
Tel: 01788 573 241
e-mail: enquiries@national.relate.org.uk
Website: www.relate.org.uk

*In Northern Ireland:*
76 Dublin Road
Belfast BT2 7HP

Tel: 028 9032 3454

*Provides a confidential counselling service for relationship problems of any kind. Local branches are listed in the phone book.*

# Working Families' Tax Credit
Helpline: 0845 609 5000
Northern Ireland helpline: 0845 609 7000
Hard of hearing helpline: 0845 606 6668
Website: www.inlandrevenue.gov.uk/wftc

*Gives information on the Working Families' Tax Credit (WFTC).*

## Parenting Courses

### Parentalk Parenting Course

A new parenting course designed to give parents the opportunity to share their experiences, learn from each other and discover some principles of parenting. For more information, phone 020 7450 9073.

### Positive Parenting

Publishes a range of low-cost, easy-to-read, common-sense resource materials that provide help, information and advice. Responsible for running a range of parenting courses across the UK. For more information, phone 023 9252 8787.

### Parent Network

For more information, call Parentline Plus on 0808 800 2222.

# More About Paren**T**alk

Launched in 1999, in response to research which revealed that one in three parents feel like failures, Parentalk is all about inspiring parents to make the most of their vitally important role.

A registered charity, we exist to provide relevant information and advice for mums and dads in a format that they feel most comfortable with, regardless of their background or family circumstances.

Our current activities include:

- **The Parentalk Parenting Principles Course**
  Already used by almost 25,000 mums and dads, this video-based resource brings together groups of parents to share their experiences, laugh together and learn from one another. Filmed at the studios of GMTV, endorsed by the National Confederation of Parent Teacher Associations and featuring Parentalk Founder Steve Chalke, the course is suitable for use by groups of parents in their own homes or by schools, PTAs, preschools and nurseries, health visitors, health centres, family centres, employers, churches and other community groups.

- **Parentalk Local Events**
  Looking at every age group from the toddler to the teenage years, and from how to succeed as a parent to how to succeed as a grandparent, Parentalk evenings are a specially tailored, fun mixture of information, shared stories and advice for success as a mum, dad or grandparent. Operating across the country, the Parentalk team of speakers can also provide

input on a range of more specialist subjects such as helping your child sleep or striking a healthy balance between work and family life.

- **Parentalk at Work Events**
Parentalk offers lunchtime and half-day workshops for employers and employees, at their place of work, that look at getting the balance right between the responsibilities of work and those of a family. Parentalk also provides a life coaching service for employees, helping them to deal with the pressures they encounter at home in order to be happier, and perform better, at work.

  All Parentalk at Work initiatives are backed up by a comprehensive website: **www.parentalk.co.uk/atwork**

- **The Parentalk Guide Series**
In addition to the 'How to Succeed' series, Parentalk offers a comprehensive series of titles that look at a wide variety of parenting issues. All of these books are easy to read, down to earth and full of practical information and advice.

- **The Parentalk Schools Pack**
This resource, designed especially for year 9 pupils, builds on the success of the Parentalk Video Course, to provide material for eight lessons on subjects surrounding preparing for parenthood. The pack has been tailored to dovetail with the PHSE and citizenship curriculum and is available for teachers to download from the Parentalk website.

- **www.parentalk.co.uk**
A lively, upbeat site exclusively for parents, packed with fun ideas, practical advice and some great tips for making the most of being a mum or dad.

To find out more about any of these Parentalk initiatives or our plans for the future, or to receive our quarterly newsletter, contact a member of the team at the address below:

**Parentalk**
**115 Southwark Bridge Road**
**London SE1 0AX**
**Tel: 020 7450 9073**
**Fax: 020 7450 9060**
**e-mail: info@parentalk.co.uk**

**Helping parents make the most of every stage of their child's growing up.**

*(Registered Charity No: 1074790)*